JOE
LAVALLY
and the
PALEFACE

JOE LAVALLY
and the
PALEFACE
in Algonquin Park

BERNARD WICKSTEED

JOE LAVALLY
and the
PALEFACE
in Algonquin Park

Originally published in 1948 by Wm. Collins Sons & Co. Ltd., Toronto.

Reprinted in 1993 by The Friends of Algonquin Park, Box 248, Whitney, Ont., K0J 2M0.

The second printing of this book was made possible by:
- a friend of The Friends of Algonquin Park
- Joel Schneider and Dr. Edmond La B. Cherbonnier

Net proceeds from the sale of this book will help to further the work of The Friends of Algonquin Park (a non-profit, charitable organization dedicated to enhancing the educational and interpretive programs in Algonquin Park).

ISBN 0–921709–85–4

PREFACE

What are you going to find in this book? I'll tell you before you start and then if you don't like the idea you needn't bother to read it. Basically it's a job reporting and what it reports is an eight-day canoe trip in the Canadian woods that I made with an Indian guide in 1945. If that's a thing you'd like to do yourself, go ahead and read the book because it's a faithful report, though I can't guarantee everything that Lavally said.

But I hope you'll find more in it than that. I hope you'll find something pleasing and helpful in the impish spirit and refreshing philosophy of the Indian who took civilisation in his stride and wasn't spoiled by it.

When I set out on the trip I took a notebook to get down local colour in case I ever wanted to write a story with a Canadian background. And how glad I was I did, because I soon found I was alone in the woods with a wit, an illiterate savant who spoke hardly a word that wasn't worth recording.

I didn't like to take notes in his presence. I was afraid he'd either dry up or turn self-conscious and silly. So I had to keep retiring to the bush, as if answering the call of nature, and there hastily scribble down as much of what he said as I could remember. As our friendship grew I retired so often that Joe commented: "You sure do suffer from innergestion. I never knew a man who had it so bad."

These notes were turned into the MS. for a book and then, when I'd finished, I learned that Joe Lavally was dead. So I made some revisions and what began as the report of a canoe trip became also the obituary of a Red Indian.

B. W.

5

CHAPTER I

JOE LAVALLY and his Brother Mat went into the woods early after the autumn to stock up their cabins for the trapping season. It had been a good summer for both of them, guiding campers and fishermen in the Algonquin Park at five dollars a day, but the real money, the thousand-dollar cheques, came with the winter when the cold of Canada thickened the coats of the beaver and mink, the fox and the fisher. Guiding was as pleasant a way as any of passing the in-between season of summer but now, with the freezing of the lakes and the first fall of snow, the fur fever was upon them and they were impatient to get their supplies laid in and their traps overhauled.

Joe worked hard with the bulky packs all day, but when they reached the first of the chain of cabins, half hidden by the spruce and balsam at the lakeside, he went straight to his bunk and rolled a cigarette, leaving Mat to light the stove.

"It's my innergestion botherin' me again," he said.

"Better take something for it," advised Mat.

Joe mixed a pinch of baking soda in a cup of snow water and took it as a draught. It relieved the pain, but he reckoned he would turn in early so as to be fit for the morning, as there was much to do.

Mat made breakfast and then called Joe. He called him twice and, getting no response, went over to the bunk and shook his brother by the shoulder. But Joe had passed on in the night to happier hunting-grounds.

It took Mat all that day and most of the night to

carry the body out to Whitney, on the Madawaska River. Round the stoves of the township's stores men said, "Did you hear about Joe Lavally? Mat just brought him in dead."

They buried him as a Catholic and, with the atomic age drawing across the headlines, no one outside Whitney thought much more about the death of this Indian trapper.

* * * * * *

As a matter of fact Joe Lavally (or Lavallée) was only half Indian. His mother was a full-blooded Algonquin and his father a French carpenter. But Joe was brought up as an Indian and always spoke of himself as one. And no one who'd seen him ever thought of him as anything else.

The summer that he and I made our canoe trip together he looked about 30 years old and said he was 56. This would be about right, people said, as he was 52 the year before. Joe couldn't read and he thought of figures as conveniences in a way of life to which he only partly subscribed. His father, he said, lived to be 104; his Indian mother 101 and her father 115. His white grandfather did not reach three figures because he was kicked to death by a horse at 80, but there was an aunt of 106 still alive and a sister "who looked 20 and was pretty near 90."

Joe himself had four grandchildren, and the British Military Medal, collected in World War I, in which he was a sniper. He was fond of saying that he had once been a guide in the Royal Canadian Mounted Police, but the Mounties, when I wrote to them, hadn't heard of him. He left the Force, he said, after a gun battle with a criminal. Having survived the war, he didn't fancy being killed "by some Jeezly old murderer."

8

He was a flying fire ranger once and sat beside the pilot looking for tell-tale wisps of smoke in the woods below. He gave that up because "his system inquired exercise" and sitting in an aeroplane all day didn't answer the inquiry. Guiding was always a good stand-by in the summer until he went to jail and had his licence suspended for ten years. He was jailed for punching a Park ranger in the jaw but when he came out, three months later, he found a job at a Jewish summer camp, teaching boys to make birch bark canoes and wigwams. They dressed him up in Indian clothes with a feather head-dress and called him "Chief." That was the part he couldn't stand. It was "Chief, this" and "Chief, that" all day long until in the end his head rang and he couldn't sleep at night for hearing childish voices calling "Chief, Chief, Chief." This, and the fact he didn't get any bacon or lard all the summer through led him to sever his connection with the Jewish camp.

When the second world war came, Joe made a great decision. He left the woods just as the trapping season was coming on and went to work as an electrician's mate in a synthetic rubber factory at Sarnia, Ontario. He gave that up because he couldn't bear the smell and volunteered to go to China to build airfields. The ship he was to have sailed on was torpedoed. "The people was saved," he said, "but all their tools and machinery was drownded."

Sixty miles north of his trap line the Government were putting up a new war plant at Chalk River and Joe made good money hauling timber for the buildings, without knowing anything of the atom bomb or the part that Chalk River was to play in its development. His contract finished, he returned to the woods and his trapping, quite unaware that in his small way he had helped introduce to the world of to-day something just as revolutionary as the coming of the white man had been to the world of his mother's people.

His guiding licence was restored to him and he resumed the old routine. In the summer it was the tourists in Algonquin Park, in the autumn the deer hunters, then, until Christmas, it was trapping. After the New Year the deep snow made trapping difficult so Joe went to work for the lumber companies until March. April was his month off, when he took his wife to the city. It was about the only time of the year when they saw each other for more than a few hours. What did an Indian and his wife, who is white, do in a big city? "We sit in fancy restaurants," he told me. "We visits people I have guided in the summer and we takes in a show and in between we go back to our room for a lie down. It costs plenty money, but my wife likes it and it's our time together."

I, the Paleface, first came into the story sitting alone in the bar of the Governor Clinton Hotel, New York, on VJ Day plus one, with a hang-over caused, not so much by the night before as by the past six years of flying, fighting, junketing and travel at Government expense. Now they were over and ahead lay the prospect of returning to the saltmines of suburban respectability. In a few weeks I should be going back to England, changing my R.A.F. uniform for a civvy suit, catching the same train to the office, the same train home, sitting at a desk wearing spectacles and trying to take an interest in matters that had come to seem trifling and futile.

I beckoned the waiter over for another drink and, feeling in my pocket for the money, pulled out a leaflet I'd forgotten was there. I'd taken if from a rack in the offices of the Canadian National Railways the day before. Outside the streets had been full of singing, dancing people celebrating the end of the war and the leaflet in my pocket went unheeded.

Now I spread it out on the table and after one minute's reading I knew what I wanted to do more than anything else in the world.

The leaflet was about the Algonquin Park game reserve in Ontario and it brought back all the longings of boyhood for a canoe trip in the Canadian wilds—Indians, trappers, moose, beavers and all that. A schoolboy in England can only read and dream of these things and as he grows up the fetters of civilisation thicken and dull the resolve to escape.

Now the whole thing seemed easy, sitting there in the New York bar with this Algonquin Park brochure on the table.

"Game is abundant," I read. "Bear and moose are occasionally encountered. Beaver, mink, marten, muskrats and practicaly all the fur-bearers are fairly common. . . . . Speckled trout run four to six pounds and are best in the Petawawa-Oxtongue River system. . . . Lake trout up to 35 pounds are caught in Opeongo and Smoke Lakes. Black bass . . . up to five pounds in the waters of the Madawaska . . . 2,000 lakes and nearly all of them contain game fish . . . ."

Even if you're no fisherman isn't there music in those names? Don't they make you want to bring out your boyhood copy of Hiawatha and read again of the Big Sea Gitche Gumee, of Pau-Puk-Keewis, the fool, and Mudwayaushka, the sound of water on the shore?

I read on: "Guides are all old-timers with as much as 25 years' experience in the Park and in bush life generally. They know the best fishing-grounds, when to fish them and how, the best type of lures and tackle. They know how to cook and make the camp comfortable and *some of them are Indians* . . . ."

The leaflet had a map of the Park and the itinerary of a suggested canoe trip from Cache Lake to Big Trout Lake which started as follows:

"Cache Lake, to Madawaska River, to Tanamakoon Lake, portage six chains to Lily Pond, portage one chain to Little Island Lake . . . ."

Apart from the names, the word portage was a nostalgic reminder of the exploits of boyhood heroes as they carried their canoes through the woods till they found navigable water again.

The waiter came up and asked if I wanted another drink. It took several seconds to get things adjusted. What was a New York waiter in a white coat doing on the portage to Little Island Lake?

"No," I said to him when I straightened things out. "I don't want another drink. I want a telephone."

That is how it all began. There was the Algonquin Park but a day's journey north with Indians, moose and 35-pound trout laid on, and there was I with 11 days' leave. Eleven days before I must report back to Washington for transportation home.

This was Wednesday. On Thursday night I was at the Highland Inn, Algonquin Park, asking the manager to find me an Indian guide. He shook his head sadly. There just weren't any, he said. Most of them were in the Army or Government war plants and the few that he had on his list were either booked or away in the woods. To prove it he pulled out a card index and shuffled through, shaking his head at each new card. "All gone," he said. "Gone or booked." Almost at the end of the index he hesitated and took out one of the cards.

From over the top of his spectacles he looked me up and down, the guest who hadn't booked, who was going back to England in a few days and whom he'd never see again. His hotel was full of holiday makers from the cities of Canada and the States who came back to him year after year and many of them wanted guides. He fingered the card lovingly, as a man who had thought himself without money and then found a note in his pocket. There was no reason in the world why Ed Paget should have given me that guide. Yet he did, and that is how I came to meet Joe Lavally.

"He's about the best man in the Park," I was told, "*and* he's the most amusing. You could write a book about Joe."

Well, Ed Paget, that is more or less what I have done.

Joe wore no feathers when he came into the manager's office, and except for a pink handkerchief round his neck, he was dressed more soberly than most of the hotel guests. But he was an Indian all right. His mother's race was stamped all over his brown unwrinkled face, on the high cheekbones and the boyish back hair. His merry dark eyes twinkled good humour and his smile made everyone else smile, too.

Joe agreed to go with me for an eight-day trip into the woods and we cemented the deal with firewater drunk from glasses over the wash basin in my room.

"We will go to my tent and disgust more about this trip," Joe said, looking at the now empty bottle and running the tip of his tongue round his lips to get the last taste.

As we went through the lobby guests looked up from their magazines and called, "Hullo, Joe," "Howya, Joe," and Joe, with me bringing up the rear, bowed and smiled and waved his hand like a potentate among his subjects.

His tent was among a clump of trees a hundred yards from the hotel and that short walk was a foretaste of things to come. A shadowy form, half the height of a man, moved silently across the path ahead and disappeared in the darkness.

"Bear," said Joe, in the tone of a man used to meeting bears in the dark.

"Made a pet of it once, but my wife didn't like him putting his head through the tent flap at night. Wouldn't harm a child, that bear, but women is funny about these things."

A deer took fright somewhere near and went off down the motor road with a clatter of hoofs. "They hangs around the hotel all the summer," said Joe. "The visitors spoils 'em. The bears is spoiled too. They get so fat on garbage they's too lazy to turn a log for theirselves."

"Why should a bear want to turn a log for himself?" I asked.

"Why, sir, he turns a log to get at the ants and bugs underneath, of course."

Joe had his wife living in the tent with him at that time. She had taken a job looking after the linen at the hotel so as to be near her husband. Even so she didn't see much of him, for nine days out of ten he was in the bush. Her father was French and her mother came from either Liverpool or London, I don't know which, because Joe said one the first time he told me and the other the next. She was sitting on one of the two brass bedsteads in the tent knitting when we called and looked as little like a grandparent as Joe. From under a pillow she brought out a bottle of raspberry wine and we drank it from cups while Joe fumbled under the other bed and produced a cigar box filled with fishing lures and knick-knacks. From it he took a spoon bait of silver which, he said, he made from a cigarette case taken off a dead German.

"Clever people, Germans," said Joe. "Clever but ugly."

He took out one of those barrel-shaped gadgets that come in half and contain bradawls, gimlets, and other tools. I had one myself as a boy, but I let Joe show me how the tools fitted into the side of the case, which then became a handle.

"Took that off a dead German, too," he said. "Clever people to think of a thing like that."

At over 50, Joe drew as much pleasure from this gadget as I had done at 15.

He brought out a map, and though he couldn't read the names, he knew every lake by its shape. There was Lobster Lake, close to where he had his winter headquarters, Straight Shore Lake, Long Bow Lake, Loontail, Moccasin and Otterpaw Lakes, all of them perfect little picture signs on the map. It was easy to see how they acquired their names.

This was Thursday night, and we arranged to start our trip on Saturday morning. We could not go on Friday because Joe was already booked to take out a guest for a day's fishing. He gave me the map and left the route to me. "We'll go where you like," he said. "Only no long portages. They're the devil. Last trip I took a party over to Lake La Muir on a portage that was two miles long. When you've walked two miles with your head inside a canoe, you're nearly drowned. There's no air."

I spent the next day sitting in the woods behind the hotel, working out a route on the map. The way I chose would take us through 40 miles of the Park, across 12 lakes, over 15 short portages and along three creeks. Joe was pleased with my choice when I showed it to him on his return in the evening. He had covered most of the territory earlier in the year, and said it was easy going. "When I was that way last," he remarked, "we didn't see another canoe for two weeks on end."

We went to the store to hire camping gear and buy our grubstakes. Most people do this in advance, so that everything is waiting for them when they step off the train, but with me the boyhood dream had turned to reality at such short notice that everything had to be done at the last minute. Consequently, we had to take what we could get and it wasn't much.

Owing to war-time rationing being still in force, there was no bacon. A bad blow this, because all the heroes of my young reading days took a hunk of bacon into the wilds. That and a flask of gunpowder were all they needed to support life on their expeditions. Nor was there any corned beef, or cooking fat. We were allowed one pound of butter, one pound of sugar and a tin of jam. There was plenty of canned beef-stew in the store, but Joe said it was heavy to carry on portages, and would let me buy only six tins. For the rest, we took five loaves of bread, flour, tea, matches, salt and a huge cabbage. Joe insisted on the cabbage, and I couldn't think why until the next day when I saw him pulling off the leaves and wrapping them round the butter.

"The bushman's refreezerator," he said. We never did eat the cabbage, but it kept our butter solid on the hottest day.

16

The grub didn't look much when it was all spread out, but Joe said it would do as we would be living mainly on the fish we caught. That suited me, for it would foster the feeling that we were living on the country, as all the best explorers do. For kit we took a tent, four blankets, frying-pan, billy-can, saucepan, plates, cups and cutlery. The only tent we could get was a large one, 12 feet by 10 feet with 3-foot walls. I said it would be all right if it rained, but Joe said that was just when it would be all wrong.

"How you'se going to carry it when it's wet?" he asked. "If the rain gets on that tent, it's going to weigh more'n the packs and the canoe put together. Yes, sir, that's a bad tent for wet weather, and there's some of it coming."

It was a beautiful summer evening when he said this. There had been hardly a cloud in the sky for days and the forecast said: "Fair and Warm," so I asked him how he knew there was a break coming.

"I was watching the loons out on the lake to-day," he answered. "They know it's going to rain. Not still for a minute, they weren't. Taking off the water and landing again and flying round uneasy, just like they always does when there's bad weather coming. Some people who hasn't studied the bush as they ought, say the loons is showing off. They gets so used to the radio and the telegraphs telling 'em all about the weather that they can't read the simplest signs Nature writes out for 'em."

In spite of the loons, the next day dawned fine and clear as forecast.

We had arranged for a truck driver to take us from the hotel to our starting-point. Joe was waiting outside with our kit laid on the grass. There were three heavy packs, the tent, two fishing-rods and the canoe.

17

He had chosen the canoe the night before, testing several of them for lightness and balance before finding one that satisfied him. It was 14 feet long and painted green with "Highland Inn" lettered on the bow, like the name of a ship.

Canoe Lake, six miles away, was our starting point, and the truck took us through the woods till the trees parted and before us lay a narrow arm of the lake, with lilies round the edge and ducks swimming in the distance. The wooded hills kept every breath of wind from the water so that the surface lay still and glossy. We unloaded on a little beach of sand and shingle, the truck drove away and we were alone in the woods —just Joe the Algonquin, and I.

The canoe had been badly bumped on the ride, and we found a tear in the canvas an inch long.

"Can't go places in a Chrysly old canoe with a hole in it," said Joe. He examined the tear carefully, spat on it and rubbed the dirt away. "It'll mend," he said, and going up to a balsam tree, cut away a pimple of gum with his knife and brought it back to the canoe. He mixed it with some of our precious cabbage-cooled butter, and stirred the result into a tacky mass which he kept fluid by the flame of a match. When the desired consistency was reached, he smoothed the mixture over the tear and left it to dry.

The whole process took less than five minutes, but the canoe did not let in one drop of water throughout the trip, though we dragged it over rocks, sunken trees and countless beaver dams.

There was no reason to linger further. We launched the canoe among the lily pads and loaded our gear —the heaviest pack in the middle, the two lighter ones at each end. I took my seat in the bow, Joe gave a shove, and we were off—off into the woods with a canoe-load of supplies and eight days of freedom ahead.

CHAPTER II

FOR half a mile we paddled up the narrow arm and then came out in the open waters of Canoe Lake with the morning sun beaming down from an almost cloudless sky. I tried to feel excited. I was in a canoe, going off into the Canadian wilds with an Indian. I had dreamed about this since I was ten years old and first read Hiawatha. Now the dream was coming true, but instead of excitement, I felt as if I had been doing it all my life. Rhythmically, I drove the paddle down, watched the water swirl and then drip from the blade as it came up for another stroke. No need to talk, for there was too much to see and feel to bother with questions. The gurgle of the water as it rippled along the sides of the laden canoe was speech enough in those first few minutes. The mirrored image of the surrounding woods, shimmering along the edges of the lake, was too beautiful, too absorbing, to allow room in the mind for thoughts in any other language but the wordless one of Nature. The water on which we moved, dulled-silver in the shadow and burnished in the sun, belonged to a world so different to the one of bombs and roaring engines in which I'd lived for six years that it seemed the very epitome of peace. And I had been spared to enjoy it. Up there, in the Airman's Valhalla of Happy Landings, were so many who had not been spared. It could be that they were looking down on me now. The crack Luftwaffe Oberst and his crew whom my pilot and I sent to their deaths off the coast of Cornwall, a beautiful flier with every trick at his fingertips, and we so raw and inexperienced. By all the rules of war and life, it was not he and his men who should have died, but us. There was the bomber crew we surprised in the dark, when they thought they were almost home. They flew through the night so confidently, so certain that they had shaken us off and that supper and bed lay ahead. As we stalked them by radar from behind, I was the most frightened man in the sky, for I had forgotten to bring my parachute. But it was they who died. And there were friends of mine, too, better men than I, more loved and loving. . . . .

I was shaken from my reverie by the painful fact that the unaccustomed excercise of paddling was making my arms ache, and that if I wasn't careful I would very soon have a blister between my right thumb and forefinger.

We had been on the water only half an hour, we had not gone more than a couple of miles, and here was I, the great explorer, getting a blister on my paddling hand.

I tried holding my thumb along the paddle handle instead of round it, and that eased things a bit. I also slowed down the *tempo* of my paddling, and presently found a pace and a degree of effort that I hoped I could keep up all day. Joe in the back was doing the real work. At best, I was only helping to keep the canoe straight.

As we continued up the lake, I discovered we were being followed by half a dozen yellow-painted canoes.

Joe said they came from a boys' camp near by, and were probably going on a camping expedition like ourselves. It was humiliating to find that the boys were gaining on us. So, ignoring my blister and arm ache, I helped Joe put on more speed to shake them off and we reached the end of the lake half a mile in front. Here we had to get out and carry the canoe and kit round a dam.

A man and a woman watched us with interest and asked how far we were going. "Off for eight days," said Joe. "Way into Big Trout Lake." "Good luck," said the man. "Wish I was coming with you." I felt I was really going places.

By this time the first of the boys' canoes was grating on the shingle and I noticed it was packed with as much kit as ours. Two boys and a youth of eighteen jumped out. The man and woman asked, "How far are *you* going?" and to my dismay one of the boys, who couldn't have been more than ten answered, "Big Trout Lake."

"What, all of you?" asked the man.

"Oh, we're only half the party," said the boy cheerfully, pointing to five more canoes just arriving. "There are another six ahead."

Allowing three to a canoe, two little and one big, there were going to be 36 boys travelling the same day, the same way and the same lake as ourselves.

In an aside to Joe I said, "I thought we were going where we wouldn't see another canoe from one day's end to another."

"Well, sir," he whispered back, "when you says this trip is a schoolboy dream of yours come true I didn't reckon on you bringing the rest of the school with you."

A few hundred yards after leaving the dam we came to a road that led down to the lakeside. Four men there were loading up two canoes, on one of which was an outboard motor. Joe hailed them and asked where they were bound. I need hardly add that the answer was Big Trout Lake. So that made 36 boys, four men, an outboard motor and us. No creature was going to stay in sight with a cavalcade like that going by; and it was wild life I had come to see, not little boys.

Joe said we had better let them all get well ahead, so we paddled to the shore and got out to stretch our legs. While I was filling my pipe Joe suddenly said he had just remembered something and walked off through the trees. He was gone more than an hour and I spent most of the time watching a black and white woodpecker digging in a rotten tree for grubs. Our commonest woodpeckers in England are green with red heads and they fly in jerks, as though one cylinder was missing. I wondered if American woodpeckers were the same or if they flew on all four cylinders. This fellow, however, was too busy hunting bugs to give a flying demonstration. I clapped my hands and shouted to make him fly away, but he took not the slightest notice. I threw sticks at him, then stones. I climbed on a stump and danced like a madman, waving my arms and shouting to make the wretched bird fly. In the midde of this performance Joe reappeared.

He must have thought I was crazy and I was expecting some wisecrack, but instead of commenting on my odd behaviour he held up two parcels and said, "See what I got."

Unwrapping the parcels he produced a four-pound

slab of bacon, a pound of dripping in a jam jar and two dozen eggs.

"Where on earth did you get all that?" I exclaimed, for with peace only four days old such things were a luxury anywhere.

"Well," he said, as if it were sufficient explanation, "I knew the woman."

Pressed for more details he continued: "I went in the back door and I see the husband and I says, 'How are me and my partner for a bit of bacon?' He says, 'You better see the wife,' so I finds her and sits down on a chair and says, 'You're not going to let me go out into the bush without a bit of bacon and some lard are you?' She says she hasn't enough for herself, let alone every Indian that comes walking in at the door. Well, sir, I been in situations like that before and I know women like a bit of fun. I says, 'Now come and sit on my knee,' and she slaps my face and then goes and gets the bacon. She says she hasn't got no lard but would dripping do? And then she fetches the eggs which I didn't ask for and tells me I'm a wicked old man."

With the lake to ourselves we continued our journey. Joe was reckoning on making 12 miles that day, which would take us to the end of Burnt Island Lake where he knew there were three camp sites. This was the first I had heard of special sites for camps. In all the books I'd read you made your camp where you wished. But that is not so in the Algonquin Park. To reduce the ever-present danger of fire, special sites have been cleared at convenient places for campers and fitted with such modern conveniences as stone fireplaces and rough-hewn tables.

There is no law against making your own site, but

it means cutting down trees and clearing the brush, not to mention building your own fireplace and table. This involved work which Joe was not prepared to do if it could be avoided.

It seemed probable, now, that by hanging back we had lost our chance of getting into any of the three camp sites at the far end of Burnt Island Lake. Joe particularly wanted to stay there for the night as the fishing was good and he suggested we should put our back into the paddling and overtake the boys ahead. So the rest of our journey that day became something of a race. For five miles our route led through a string of narrow lakes called respectively Joe Lake, Little Joe Lake and Baby Joe Lake. Half-way up the first of them we overhauled one of the canoes. The two small boys in front were beginning to tire, and most of the work was being done by the big lad in the stern. Joe said he was called a councillor—or would it be counsellor? On such trips as these boys were making there was always one councillor to each canoe. They were mostly college boys on vacation and had the privilege of doing most of the work, carrying the canoe on the portages and deciding where to camp.

Our first real portage came between Little Joe and Baby Joe. It was only a hundred yards, but a good rehearsal for the longer ones ahead. We dumped all the kit out on the shore and pulled up the canoe. Joe tied the two paddles inside, lengthways between the centre seats and a foot apart. Then with a mighty heave he turned the canoe upside down and hoisted it over his head, so that the two paddles rested one on each shoulder. His back curved and his knees bent under the weight as he staggered up the bank and disappeared between the trees.

24

I managed to get two of the packs on my back, one balanced on the other. In trying to pick up the fishing-rods the second pack overbalanced and fell with a crash, just missing the eggs. I got it back again with some difficulty and decided to call two packs a load. They weighed over a hundred pounds between them, I should think, and one of the straps almost cut my collar bone in two before I even started. By the time I had stumbled the hundred yards to the next lake the strap was hurting so much that I wondered if I would ever have the use of my right arm again. The offending strap, I found, had a large strip off it, as if someone had cut it with a knife. Joe, resting after carrying the canoe, examined it and said some camper had left the pack out all night and rabbits had made a meal off the strap. This was the first time I had ever heard rabbits were not strict vegetarians. I have eaten leather myself. It goes by different names, but I don't remember the waiter ever calling it lettuce.

Later on, Joe and I got this portaging business down to a fine art. He took the canoe and went right through with it. I took two packs half-way, dumped them beside the track and then returned for the rest, which I carried right through. In the meantime Joe came back half-way and picked up the first load. In this manner we each made one and a half loaded trips.

It worked fairly well, and would have been perfect if there had been some infallible way of telling just when I had reached the half-way mark. Sometimes I misjudged it so badly that I went almost the whole way with the first load, and that annoyed me because I had done more work than I need. Once or twice I uderestimated it and that annoyed Joe, because he had to do more than his share. I always knew

25

from the map the rough length of the portage before I started, but walking down a path on which you have never set foot before, bent almost double under your load, and unable to see more than a few feet ahead, makes it difficult to judge distances. I tried counting my spaces, but they varied widely, according to the nature of the surface, and the results were erratic.

Our first portage took us into Baby Joe Lake, which is no more than a mile or so in length. It was then one o'clock and we reckoned we would have lunch at the other end, before portaging again into Burnt Island. We scrapped the idea when we got there and found five canoe-loads of boys having their lunch. Joe said we would go through and eat at the other end of the portage, but there were three canoes and nine more boys there. So we launched the canoe and paddled on till we came to a wooded headland where Joe said we would stop.

A shelving rock ran in a gentle slope from the water to the trees, inviting travellers to stay and rest. While Joe lit a fire I went off to seek out wild life. All I saw was an angry-sounding red squirrel who seemed to take a very poor view of my intrusion. It was the first red squirrel I had seen since a boy. At home in England our squirrels have been Americanised beyond recognition. The transformation is said to have begun when several American grey squirrels escaped into Regent's Park from the London Zoo. They took to the place like G.I.'s to Piccadilly, and soon there weren't any native red squirrels left. The conquest of London complete, they swarmed into the country, like Yankee carpet-baggers invading the South after the Civil War, so that now the only places in which you will see a red squirrel in the British Isles are the inaccessible extremities. If squirrels ever learn to drive jeeps, and I wouldn't put it beyond the American variety, even those last fastnesses of native squirreldom may be doomed. The two don't mix. They are a different genus and cannot even fraternise, for they are, biologically, more different from each other than the horse and the donkey. One of them has to go and at the moment the red squirrel, like the red man, is getting the worst of it.

The little squirrel of the Canadian woods chattered away in his high squeeky little voice, jumping from branch to branch to keep up with me. He was like those members of the human race who cannot speak without using their hands, but in his case it was his tail. Every time he opened his mouth he shook his tail. I thought at first he was wild with me, but thinking it over he may have been saying that, though his cousins in Britain had perished, he was keeping the flag flying in the Empire.

Joe had heated one of the tins of stew and made a pail of tea when I returned. We ate and drank sitting on the rock in the sun, and, my word!—that tea was good, black as pitch and scalding hot, with the aroma of wood smoke curling from the cup. I had four cupfuls. What opium does to Chinamen and marijuana to South Americans, wood-smoked tea does to me. It exhilarates, it intoxicates, it brings complete forgetfulness of civilisation and its complications.

Joe didn't like the sun and the rock we were sitting on grew too hot for him, so he moved to the shade of a tree. But I lay back and relaxed with my eyes closed. The camp-fire smell stole into my senses like a woman's perfume and I thought, "Why don't I always live like this? What is the sense in cities, toiling to make money for other people, held by convention to the grindstone so as to earn enough to pay some profiteering landlord for the privilege of living in his brick prison?"

If the decision to revolt and go native was one that could be made in an instant I would have made it then, at my first halt in the summer woods with Joe.

But this train of thought was disturbed by the reappearance of the boys, who came paddling past our headland in full song, splashing the water with their paddles and yelling in chorus. Joe, dozing in the shade with his back against a tree, jumped to his feet and said we must be going. Otherwise we would lose our camp site.

The last canoe-load of boys was past us and out of sight before we were ready to start again, so once more we had the whole field ahead. This time I asked Joe whether he minded if I paddled on the left, so as to rest my blistered right hand. He said he would prefer it. He could paddle either side equally well, but just now he had rheumatism in the shoulder and right-hand paddling was easiest. Somehow, I had never thought of Indians having rheumatism. It is not a subject you come across in cowboy stories. Joe said he got it in the summer only. In the winter, when the weather was dry and cold, he was all right. Because of his rheumatism he wore thick woollen underclothes. The doctor had sent him a set, but they scratched so much he said he wouldn't wear them. So the doctor sent him some others that were better. Then he had the first set washed, and after that they were better too, so now he had two sets. But he wore them in the summer only. As soon as the cold weather came, he took them off and hired them to another man for the winter.

As we paddled along the lake in the sunshine, I got on to the subject of moose and our chances of seeing one. I promised him that if we did, I would give him my American Army pattern boots, which he coveted. He was confident he would win them, but I must not be disappointed if the moose we saw did not have its full spread of antlers, because "they were wearing velvet" at that time of year.

An important question then arose, which was this: Do porcupines eat a moose's antlers?

It arose this way. The mention of "velvet" had reminded me that many kinds of deer shed their antlers once a year, and in the mountains of Norway I have found those of reindeer lying on the ground. So I asked Joe if discarded moose horns were ever found in the bush. Without hesitation, he replied, "Very seldom" and continued as follows:

"You don't find them because the old porcupine eats 'em. Yes, sir, if a porcupine finds one of those moose 'cups' in the bush, he pretty near camps beside it till it's finished. You hear him chawing away there all night. There's people who will say when they hear it, 'That old porcupine has a hard bit of wood to chaw,' but I know it is moose cups he's chawing, because I've seen him at it."

At the time I thought this rather a nice little nature story, not the kind you read in books, but first-hand observation by the man on the spot; and it was announced with such conviction and picturesque detail that it never occurred to me to doubt it.

But what do the scientists say? When I returned to London I wrote out a questionnaire on some of the biological points raised by Joe, and this business of the porcupine's diet was on the list. I stated the case and asked, "Does this sound reasonable?" Then I sent the whole thing off to the London Zoo.

The completed questionnaire came back by return post with a courteous covering note from Dr. Edward Hindle, F.R.S., the Scientific Director, and written below the porcupine question was the one word "No."

So I tried a cousin of mine, Doktor Don Kuenen, of Leiden University, who is also a biologist. He said, "No" too, but he said it in more words. He said, "There are plenty of instances of animals eating the cast-off parts of other animals, but the American porcupine is a vegetarian. It lives on bark and twigs and leaves. Before answering a question like this, the scientist must ask himself, 'Why should the porcupine *want* to eat moose antlers?' "

"Well," I said, "maybe he likes to cut loose once in a while. Even a porcupine may have his moments. If he has a secret passion for moose cups, why shouldn't he break out sometime?"

"That," answered Doktor Kuenen "is not what I mean, by *want*. I should have said *need*. Why does a porcupine *need* to eat moose antlers? What physical requirements would they satisfy? Why should it *need* all the lime they contain?"

I pointed out that everyone in Canada knew the porcupine had a mania for salt. It gets itself into much trouble round lumber camps and other human habitations for this very reason. So if it has a mania for salt, why not lime?

But Doktor Kuenen shook his head.

Well, there you are. Take your choice. It's either Joe, the Indian, who saw more porcupines in his life than any scientist, or the scientists, who have studied porcupines in closer detail than any Indian.

Nevertheless, if anyone happens to have a tame porcupine around the place, he might further the interests of science by trying to feed it on cast-off moose horns.

Half-way up the lake we passed a tiny island, not more than fifty yards across, on which were camped a young man and his girl. Joe said he'd seen them when he passed that way the last time, and he thought they'd been there the whole summer. They were swimming when we went by. Their canoe was pulled up on the rocks and their tent almost hidden among the trees.

There, on that little wooded island paradise, were two sensible and fortunate people. Sensible, because instead of just dreaming about living on an island together, they went out and did it, and fortunate because, having done so, they had gone through the summer without cutting each other's throats.

When their supplies ran low, they were no more than half a day's determined paddling and portaging from the railway. They could leave early in the morning, pick up fresh provisions and be back in Eden before nightfall. For the rest, they could fish, swim, and do whatever else a young man and a girl would wish to do when alone together on an island. And not just for a mere ten days or two weeks, but for a whole summer.

We were overhauling canoe loads of boys now with some regularity, but there were still many ahead. Joe said two of the camps we were all making for were on the lake shore, close to the start of the next portage, and the other on a little island a mile or so nearer. He thought that perhaps the boys wouldn't know about the island site, so we would go for that.

After seeing the bliss of the camp we had just passed, I was much in favour of islands.

Half a dozen canoes were still ahead when the promised isle came in view and four of them were on a course which was going to take them perilously near to it. As we sweated to get there first, I saw with relief one, then two, then three of them paddle past and head for the far shore. The occupants of the fourth, however, had clearly no such intentions. They were a quarter of a mile ahead and the race seemed lost. Joe said we still had a chance because they were going the wrong side. The camp site lay to the left, and they were going round on the right.

Soon the island hid them from view, and we put on an extra spurt which brought us to the landing-rock just as they reappeared round the far end. I leapt out of the canoe, ran up the soft pine-needle slope and took possession, while Joe threw our kit on the rocks. We made it by no more than 30 seconds.

In the excitement of the landing operations, I had hardly bothered to look at the site. We had got it, and it was on an island at least a mile from where anyone else could camp, and that, at the moment, seemed sufficient. But Joe, when he came up the slope with the packs, gave it a more critical survey. The first thing he noticed was that there were no tent poles and no small timber from which to cut them. The table of rough wood, nailed at one end to a pine tree and supported at the other by a pile of rocks, looked quite good to me, but displeased Joe, because it wobbled.

I didn't know then that when it came to tables, Joe was a little queer. Whatever else was wrong with the camp, the table had to be right. We didn't make a camp throughout the whole trip in which he did not either reconstruct the existing table beyond recognition or build an entirely new one. At our second camp, where we stayed for three days, he made a new table every morning after breakfast. We finished up by having breakfast at one, lunch at another and dinner at the third.

There were other things about this first camp that seemed far more wrong to me. For a start, the place was littered with paper, like Hampstead Heath the day after a Bank Holiday, or Broadway after a procession. There were rusting tins everywhere, just lying around where the openers had tossed them. I counted about 20 and then gave it up, for there were hundreds. Empty bottles, half-filled packages of salt, mouldy flour bags and bits of rag lay around.

I suggested to Joe that perhaps we had not done so well after all, and that we should go somewhere else and make a new camping-ground, but he said that would be more work than to clear up where we were.

CHAPTER III

WE had taken possession at about 4.30 p.m., and our idea had been to dump our stuff and go off to catch a fish. Then we would come back while it was still light, put up the tent and cook the fish for supper. But the camp cleaning put us back two hours in our programme. Joe didn't help much. He was too busy with his hatchet making a new table, so I picked up every one of those hundreds of tins myself and made a dump 30 yards from the camp. I gathered enough paper to win a prize in a salvage drive, and in the end the place looked quite habitable.

We were further delayed by the fish we intended eating for supper. It wouldn't get caught.

Joe told me about all the trout his clients had hooked last time he was here. They were many and large, and they just lined up to be caught. I am an old enough fisherman to know better, but tales like this still beguile me.

Our quarry was a lake trout. Not too big, said Joe. Five to ten pounds would do nicely. Over that weight they weren't so good in the pan. I have caught many trout in my life, but except for one never-to-be-forgotten day in Norway, when I landed a six-pounder, I had never taken anything over one pound and a half. So this talk about mere five- and ten-pounders was a bit out of my class.

Ed Paget at the hotel had looked at my tackle, said it was no good for these waters and lent me a copper-line outfit. He said the trout lie so deep that, however heavily weighted, an ordinary trolled line doesn't get down to them. So instead of a linen line, I now had a cumbersome one of copper wire. This sinks with its own weight. At a suitable trolling speed, and with an average type of lure, it goes down 20 feet for every 100 feet of line let out. Joe told me to put out about 150 feet, which meant we were fishing 30 feet below the surface. Some men go to twice that depth, he said.

It is possible to fish like this only if the guide knows the water well, otherwise the line will catch in rocks or shoals. The hooks then pick up muck from the bottom and look to a fish like yesterday's dinner. With all that copper wire out, the rod feels so heavy that a fisherman as unused to it as me, doesn't notice the gentle bump of the hooks touching the mudbanks on the bottom.

While we were trolling I sat on the floor of the canoe, facing Joe with my back against the seat. He told me a lot about lake trout. One of the best places to catch them was Opeongo, the largest lake in the park. As the leaflet had said, they went up to 35 pounds there and 10 pounds was a fair average. Big Trout Lake, where we were going, was full of fish, but there weren't so many large ones caught now as when the lake was given its name. With Opeongo it was the other way round. The big fellows did not appear until some years after the lake was opened up to fishermen. Years ago Joe used to take parties out there and for days on end they caught nothing over a few pounds. He became so tired of listening to people complaining that he eventually refused to guide on that lake. Then a dam was built and it raised the water level by several feet. Mysteriously, huge trout began to appear. Parties went out and caught half a dozen twenty-pounders in a few hours. Those trout, said Joe, must have been there all the time. They could not have grown to that size in a season. They were ten years old or more. Joe's explanation was that originally the fish had to go right to the bottom of the lake to find water cold enough for their tastes. When the level of the lake was raised the water was still cold enough some feet from the bottom, where they were much easier to catch.

When a lake trout gets into warm water all the fight goes out of him, said Joe. It's just as if you was to put me down in the tropics," he said. "I'd have no spirit. I couldn't cut timber nor carry a 200-pound pack all day. It's the same with the old trout. He likes it best when there's ice about and plenty of cold. That's what he's brought up to. When the summer comes and the water gets warm he has to go down deep like you and I goes and looks for a nice shady tree. He don't like warm water any more than you like warm beer."

To an Englishman in the North American continent the question of beer temperature is a sore point, so I let it pass.

We went on trolling for more than an hour without feeling anything on the line. Joe tested the tension with his hand and said he thought I had dirt on the hooks. It took some minutes to wind in 150 feet of not very pliable copper wire, and when the lure came in sight it was heavy with old leaves and sticks. How long they had been on I do not know. Most of the time the line had been out, perhaps. Judging by the look Joe gave me that is what he thought. He was the man doing all the work. My part was but to sit in the canoe with the rod in my hands and hook the fish when it took the bait. Not only had I been unsuccessful, but, in Joe's opinion, stupid as well.

After cleaning the lure I let it out again. "Slowly," said Joe. "If you let line out fast it sinks too deep."

Anxious to please, I took about five minutes to let the 150 feet go. I could only guess at it. There was no mark on the line. I reckoned one turn of the reel equalled six inches, so I counted up to 300 turns and held it at that. After five minutes something hit and I was so surprised that I struck wildly. Joe shouted, "Hey, hey, steady, you'll pull the hooks out." But the fish was there all right. I could feel that first wild lunge, then the second and the third. They were damped down by the weight and the length of the line, but they were there.

"Wind in. Keep the pressure on." said Joe, increasing his speed with the paddle.

I wound in with a steady methodical movement. After the first few charges the fish had given up the fight. The weight of one hundred and fifty feet of copper line was too much for the stout heart of even a trout. It was like pulling in an old boot filled with water. By the time I had him on the surface he didn't have enough fight left even to shy away from the canoe, and Joe, without gaff or net, took the line near his mouth and yanked him in, as nice a seven-pound trout as you'd ever wish to see. But I've had more sport with four-ounce roach on a horsehair lead.

With our supper secured we went ashore and cut five tent poles. They were longer than the canoe itself and it was quite a feat getting back to our island without upsetting. It was growing dark then, and across the lake the camp fires of the boys were twinkling on the shore.

Joe said we would cook first and put the tent up by moonlight.

While he was lighting the fire I stripped and went for a swim. And what a swim it was, naked and primeval. If any worldly cares lingered unsuspected in my system they were swept away in the plunge from the rocks. Off came the sweat and grime of a hot hard day, away went that last defiling feel of civilisation—the taint that clothing leaves on flesh. The clean clear water of that northern lake, softened by rain and warmed by the summer sun, was like Nature herself taking an errant child to her all-forgiving bosom. No mortal mother could give so comforting a caress, no woman make for her lover such a sanctuary of touch. If the ministers of God could facilitate such communion as I had in that swim their churches would always be full to the doors.

Joe had the fish cleaned, cut up and already browning in the pan when I got back to the camp. "Swimming, huh," he said with a grunt of what I took to be disapproval.

"Yes," I said, on the defensive. "And one of the best swims I've ever had in my life Back in Washington it costs a dollar fifty and there are so many people in the pool you can't move."

"Lots of young girls, I expect," said Joe.

"Yes, plenty of girls."

"And all sitting around with not much on."

"That's right. They don't wear much these days."

"Well, sir, maybe it is worth that dollar fifty just to look around."

By this time all that was left of daylight was a narrowing strip of red and purple in the west. Above and around the full darkness of night had fallen. Joe squatted over the fire, purposely made small for cooking, and turned the cutlets of fish over in the pan. The seven pounds of trout made six cutlets which he had first rolled in fat and flour. As he turned them he added salt in generous pinches. "Always put salt in the pan," he said, "so it will perment round the grease.

"It's an odd thing," he went on, "but if you cook a fish right after catching it like this, it never goes real brown in the pan. Keep it overnight and next morning you can make it as brown as a deer in spring."

Brown or not, it was superlatively good. I was for sitting on the ground and eating it round the fire, but Joe insisted we use the table and piled wood on the fire to provide the necessary illumination.

The flesh of lake trout is a delicate rose-peach, firm

38

as salmon and just as filling. Two pieces were all I could eat, which was tantalising because better fish I have seldom tasted. On the whole I do not think much of the fish in America. In the restaurants everything you order, whatever it happens to be called, has a way of turning out to be mackerel. They call it sea trout, lake trout, and half a dozen other things and each time you order hopefully. But it never varies. Sometimes it is cooked better than at others, but it is still mackerel—or was during the war.

This, however, was the real thing, and we washed it down with hot black tea and then, thoroughly gorged, sat round the fire with our backs to the trunks of convenient trees. The dishes had to be washed, the tent put up and beds of spruce laid out, but I for one, and Joe for the other, didn't intend to do anything for the moment.

A moon, more than half full, scattered silvery ripples on the water. A dozen bullfrogs had got together for a symphony concert, but had forgotten all the instruments but the double basses. Somewhere in the darkness a party of ducks on passage made wisequacks as they swam.

"I suppose this is all quite natural to you, Joe, and you think nothing of it," I said.

He answered, "Well, sir, I was born in the bush and I was raised in the bush and, until I joined the army in the first war and went to Pembroke to be trained, I'd never seen a brick house or a railroad. Since then I've seen plenty. I've seen Paris and London, I've seen a place I forget the name of that's the capital of Ireland, I've seen Montreal and New York and that place in the States where they make automobiles and you go to by bus from Sarnia. I've seen all these

39

places, and Toronto, too, and I can tell you this, sir, I wouldn't give a beaver skin, not one Jeezly beaver skin, for the whole bunch of 'em. I wouldn't give a muskrat's skin, no, nor even a wee timber weasel skin for any city you like to name.

"My wife, sir, she says to me, 'Why you always out in the bush? Why can't you stay at home for a few days instead of acting as uneasy in the house as a mouse when there's a marten around?' You can't tell a woman anything, because they don't understand. Take them out in the bush and try to let them see for themselves, and they want to go home. They say they can't stand the wolves howling or the loons calling all night, or some such nonsense. No sir, the bush is something a woman can't understand, and they haven't no patience. When I came back after the war there was a girl I was going to marry in Pembroke. I told her I was going north to save some money so we would have a good time at the wedding, and she said, 'Oh, fine.' Well, sir, up north I made 150 dollars a month summer and winter, and I stayed for three years and then came back and bought a brick house in Pembroke. Yes, a brick house, and I bought it right away, the first day I comed back. Then I went to look for the girl and she'd gone away to Ottawa with another fellow and married him. Couldn't wait three years, you see. They're like that, women are. No patience. So I went back to the bush and I've stayed there most of the time ever since. If it wasn't to give my wife a treat I'd never go near another city again."

"What about your brick house in Pembroke, Joe?"

"I rented that out to a family and they're still there. It's my house, but I never seen it since."

Which just goes to show. If there are Fifth Columnists and revolutionaries lurking undetected in our midst, there are also landlords in the most unsuspected places. I asked Joe how he met his wife. He said she was a schoolgirl the first time he saw her. She asked him the way to some place and, instead of just telling her, he escorted her there himself. A year or so later he was working on a building job with her father, putting in the foundations of a sawmill. The two of them had a common dislike for their foreman. One day Joe said to the foreman, "Why don't you put a sack over your head and get a bull to push some brains into you?"

This flow of language, somewhat richer than I have quoted it, so impressed the father that he invited Joe round to play euchre.

There were two daughters in the house. When it was time for Joe to go home the elder should have shown him to the door. Instead of that the younger, the one Joe had met before, jumped up from her chair and showed him out. The same thing happened next time he called and Joe became so intrigued that he used to let the old man win at euchre so as to make sure he would be asked again.

They had five children. "I often wish," said Joe, with a trace of wistfulness, "that we'd had a large family."

From somewhere across the lake a loon was calling to its Maker to release it from the purgatory of life on earth. There is no sound quite like a loon calling. It doesn't belong to this world. In the following week I heard hundreds of loons in the night and got to understand the way Joe said women felt about them. If you have heard the cry you will know what I mean.

If you haven't, no mere words will ever convey the full import of that unearthly sound. Most sounds you come across in life are explicable. You may not know the exact mechanics of their production, but they sound reasonable. There is none of that about the night cry of the loons. In the daytime they use another language, a bird language, but nevertheless an earthly one. It is only at night that they transcend the limits of terrestrial possibility. Perhaps if you poured boiling water down the pipes of a church organ while it was playing something particularly soulful you might get a pale reproduction of the sound I mean. It is all very painful.

Sometimes, as I lie awake in Hampstead, London, I hear the trains hooting and whistling at Willesden Junction, five miles away, and for a moment, a minutest fraction of a second, I think I hear the loons again, but the spell is soon broken, for nothing on earth but a loon can sustain such astral sound.

In daylight, it all seems absurd, like a nightmare dream dispelled by illumination, for the loon is really one of the most ridiculous birds you ever came across, a regular dodo of a bird. It can swim and fly and dive and hold its breath under water for minutes on end, but it can't do a simple thing like walk. The Great Designer placed the centre of gravity so far in front of its legs that when it tries to stand it falls forward on its neck. The only way it can progress on land is to shuffle along on its belly. This may account for the frustration and agony of its cry. In its own way, it may be calling, "Oh God, move my centre of gravity back."

Joe said a loon goes about 40 pounds. He always prefaced descriptions of people and creatures with an estimate of weight. The loons left the Canadian Lakes in the autumn, but where they went he did not know. Original research on my part, i.e., writing to the London Zoo, reveals that the Canadian loon is none other than the great northern diver of the Scottish lochs. When the lakes of Canada freeze, they migrate south to Florida and Lower California, but sometimes they take the first turning on the left and end up in Scotland, where they may have provided the original inspiration to the man who invented bagpipes.

To the accompaniment of the loons calling and the logs of driftwood crackling on the fire, Joe told me the story of "that double murder a few years back."

There was a trapper named Jack, he said, who was in trouble for poaching. A ranger and his assistant went round to his cabin to arrest him and were never seen again.

"The searchers went after them," said Joe, "and they found that trapper's cabin burned down. They raked round the ashes and picked out the bones of the two men. They knowed it was them, because they found the ranger's badge and the other guy's gold ring. There was so little left of them that they put the bones of the one into a five-quart can, and of the other into a six-quart can.

"Of course, the Mounties was greatly excited. They just filled the bush full of policemen. I said to them, 'You'll never catch a trapper like that. He knows the bush better than you ever will.' So they said, 'Well, Joe, what do you suggest?' I said to them, 'Give me one man, in ordinary clothes like a trapper would wear, and I'll take him to Jack's hiding-place. More'n one man I won't take, and I won't have no one in uniform.' So they said, 'All right, Joe. You know best. We'll do that.'

"Well, I knew where Jack was hiding all right. He had a cabin in the bush I knew about. I'd been there before, and I took that policeman right to the place. I banged on the door and shouted, 'How are we for some pancakes, Jack?' and he opened the door and said, 'Why, it's Joe.' I said, 'Yes, and hungry too, like my partner here,' meaning the policeman. He said, 'Sure, I got some pancakes for you,' and he starts to get the things to mix them with. Just as soon as his back's turned, the Mountie pulls out his gun and says: 'Put 'em up, Jack.' Well, sir, you should have seen that man's face. He turns to me and says, 'If I'd known that was your trick, there'd have been another double murder.' "

I said something about Jack not being a very nice character, to which Joe replied that he was not a really bad man. "He was simple, that's all," he said. "A bit funny in the head. And they bothered him, those rangers. They bothered him terrible. He never done no one any harm, except poach a few beaver skins, but them rangers kept following him. I told 'em Jack was a good man to leave alone. He made a poor living and never had money in the summer. If he'd been a big poacher, he'd have had money all the year, see? So why bother with him? Specially when he's a man likely to turn ugly if he's bothered too much! But they didn't listen. Only reason I helped the Mounties bring him in was I feared once he'd started killing, he might stay nasty and go on at it. Next time it mightn't have been just a couple of rangers. He might have killed a trapper. He might have killed me. Otherwise I'd never have taken them to his hiding-place."

44

This was just one of Joe's stories of his deeds with the Mounties. In the week that followed, he told me many others. I wrote them on out my return, and sent them to the headquarters of the Mounted Police in Ottawa, asking for further details. I am afraid I must report that Assistant Commissioner H. A. R. Gagnon, Director of Criminal Investigation, wrote in reply that they had no record of Joe ever having been employed by the Force, nor could they identify any of his stories with those on their files.

"We feel sure," he wrote, "that they can be regarded as a figment of this man's imagination."

Thank you, Commissioner, but figments or not, they were good camp-fire yarns, and worth repeating.

We put up the tent by moonlight. It was after ten and the fires that the boys had lit on the opposite shore had twinkled out and died and there was nothing to remind us that we were not the only people on the lake.

We cut armfuls of spruce twigs and laid them on the tent floor three or four inches thick, like mattresses. Over them we spread our blankets and put our packs at the head for pillows. Joe, with his boots off, but little else, lay on his back, hands behind his head, puffing away at a cigarette which illuminated his face with a dull red glow every time he drew. The tent was filled with the smell of fresh-cut spruce, a soothing, clean and friendly odour. "It smells even better if you mix a little balsam with the spruce," Joe said.

We discussed our plan of campaign for the next day. We could make Big Trout Lake quite comfortably, but I was in favour of a very early start so that we might pass the boys before they broke camp. Then, if we could keep ahead, we might have a chance of

45

seeing some wild life. Joe said, with some show of contempt, that we wouldn't have to get up very early to do that. He knew what these boys were like in a camp. "First they must have their swim," he said. "Then they play games and it is ten o'clock before they are away."

It had been years since I'd slept so near to mother earth, and the spruce twigs soon bedded down and became nearly as hard as the ground itself. Around midnight I gave up trying to sleep. Joe, the Indian, was breathing with the even rhythm of oblivion as I unrolled myself from the blanket and crept stealthily from the tent. There was no special reason why I should creep with stealth, but I found myself imagining I was a captured paleface escaping from a wigwam while the guard slept. Every step was taken with care and cunning. With my toe I first felt the ground before putting weight on my foot. Many a paleface of old had died through snapping a twig as he trod. I reached the entrance of the tent with no more sound than came from the pumping of my heart. I did not rustle or disturb the canvas flaps as I passed out. Not a joint creaked as I moved away on the carpet of fallen pine needles. I had escaped without waking the redskin. Then I trod on the edge of the frying-pan and the handle came up and hit me on the shin. Instinctively I recoiled, and the pan fell back with a clatter on the enamelled plates lying beside it. The row was terrific, and I expected Joe to come rushing out of the tent. When he didn't come I peeped in and listened. His breathing was as even as ever.

The moon was still in the sky and a slight mist lay in wispy patches on the water. There was a night chill about the air that drew the shoulders together, but when I climbed down the rocks and put my hand in the water, it was as warm as it had been in the afternoon sun. As if answering some call of instinct, and hardly knowing I was doing it, I slipped off my clothes and slid silently into the still, misty water.

Have you ever added to the richness of life by taking a moonlight bathe when everyone around you slept? It is a practice that almost smacks of witchcraft and black magic. I was first initiated as a boy at boarding-school. When the moon was full, the few of us the gods had chosen for the rite slipped in unspoken agreement from our dormitory beds, stole downstairs and across the playing-fields to the swimming-bath. We couldn't dive, we couldn't shout or talk or splash, for the noise would have awakened the slumbering house-masters. We just slid into the water and swam with easy unrippling strokes until the ceremony was over and it was time to return to bed.

Boys, as you know, are inclined to gang up, but we, of the moonlight bathing cult, were no gang. We weren't even specially good friends. Nothing was planned or plotted in advance or spoken of after-wards. Those of us who were chosen just answered the call. Sometimes we were discovered and punished, but it made no difference. When the call came again we were there.

A score of times since I have been bidden and obey-ed. The last occasion had been only a few months back, in Florida, when a party of R.A.F. officers had borrowed a brake and gone for a moonlight drive along the coast road out of Palm Beach. As if by in-stinct, the Wing Commander who was driving pulled to the side after passing the last house. In complete accord, we took off our uniforms and ran naked down

47

the beach to the sea. Then, after the bathe, danced on the road in the beams of our brake headlights. Five men, without a stitch of clothing between us, pranced in a circle on the macadam road, like albino aborigines calling to their gods for rain or fertility.

If any unseen observer had been spying on us from the shadows of the palms he would have thought we were cracked. Perhaps we were, but it seemed quite a natural thing to do at the time.

Now, on the Burnt Island Lake, Algonquin Park, Ontario, the call had come again, and, obeying it, I swam slowly round the island. At times the night mist swirled round my head and hid everything, and then it cleared, and the moon looked down in approval. A ridge of little rocks ran out from the head of the isle, and a family of ducks, with squatting rights for the night, splashed noisily into the water at my approach and swam in agitation for the shadows. A few hundred yards ahead an arrowhead of ripples on the water betrayed another moonlight swimmer, faster and more agile than I. An otter, a beaver, a muskrat, I don't know and never will, for at sight of me it disappeared in a swirl and I saw it no more.

The island was between a quarter and a half-mile round, and as I turned the last corner, there was something else in the water, opposite the landing-rock. Something big this time. Could it be a deer? Could it be, thrill of thrills, a moose? *The* moose, that I had come to Canada to see? I stopped swimming and dog-paddled to avoid making tell-tale ripples. Then I saw that whatever the thing was, it was coming *towards* me. I didn't know whether to turn and swim for the shadows cast on the water by the island's trees, or stay where I was and hope to be unobserved. It certainly wasn't a moose, for it had no antlers. It wasn't a deer either. It wasn't any kind of wild animal. It was man. For a moment he was lost in a wisp of mist, and then he emerged again so near that I could see it was Joe.

Joe, who had seemed to regard my earlier swim with disfavour, Joe, who had spoken with contempt of the boys who bathed before breaking camp, Joe, late of the Mounties (or not of the Mounties), Joe the trapper, guide, hunter, and timberman was a moonlight swimmer, too!

CHAPTER IV

WE didn't speak. It seemed unnecessary as we swam side by side back to the landing place. As we rubbed ourselves down, Joe said he had heard me tread on the frying-pan, but feigned sleep till he found out what was going on. When I went away again he got up and saw my clothes on the rock. After watching, and listening, for a while he heard the ducks taking fright at the far end of the island and guessed I was having a swim.

"I'm a good swimmer," he said. "But I don't do much of it now. Mostly I only swim when I change my underclothes."

However, sitting there on the moonlit rock he had felt the urge, too, taken off his clothes and followed me in.

The last thing I remember him saying, as he rolled

himself up in his blankets for the second time that night, was that he got up at six o'clock every morning of his life. So when I awoke and saw daylight through the tent flap I looked to see if he was up. Seeing he wasn't I presumed it was not yet six and turned over for another doze. Half a dozen times I did this before looking at my watch to discover that it was eight o'clock. And Joe was still asleep.

Outside, the mist had thickened since our moonlight swim and now looked the typical prelude to a scorching day. Above, the sun was trying to get through a blanket of vapour, and below, the dead calm surface of the lake mirrored the filtered light. The shore where the boys were camping was blotted out, but shouts and bursts of song showed they were still there. Nearer, the tops of trees showed through the mist like little islands floating in the air. The bushes round the camp had got themselves up with Nature's jewellery, made from spiders' webs and dew, which sparkled with the freshness of morning. From the rocks beside our canoe a party of ducks was slipping into the lake as I came out. They had little red crests which didn't show till the ducks leant forward to take the water. There were six in the family and they paddled off without alarm towards the far end of the island. Joe called them shell-ducks and said they were no good to eat because they lived on fish.

A kingfisher flew by, making uncomplimentary remarks as he passed, and behind the tent a woodpecker was getting his breakfast from the rotting wood of an old maple.

Altogether it was a scene I don't think anyone would want to miss.

Joe came out from the tent, rubbing his eyes rather

sheepishly, and looked up at a tree in which a squirrel was cracking pine kernels and dropping bits on the canvas. "Hullo," he said to the squirrel. "I guess you get a poor living on this Chrysly old island."

He went down to the water and squatted on his haunches to wash his face, and across the lake the mist drifted into little cloudlets and rose from the surface. First the white trunks of the birches showed through on the opposite shore, then the pines and finally the whole forest stood out like a picture on the wall, with the lake as the bottom of the frame, and the underside of the mist-blanket above. By the time Joe had washed and started the fire the whole sky was warm and blue and clear. You see mists clearing away on the films, sometimes, when the producer wants to be especially fancy in his scene changing. But Hollywood hasn't learnt to do it as beautifully as has nature.

Joe wasn't too pleased when he saw it was going to be hot. He had been predicting bad weather from the day before we started and seemed to feel he was on his mettle to produce it. Also a hot day meant harder work on the portages. But he cheered up when he remembered we had bacon and eggs for breakfast. He cut the bacon in thick slices with his pocket-knife and said, as he dropped them in the pan, "We're big people, eating bacon in the morning. I bet there's no one else in the Park has bacon for breakfast today."

When the slices were transparent and nearly ready he stacked them at one side of the pan and cracked in four eggs. Now I belong to the school of cookery thought which believes in cracking the egg on the edge of the pan, so I watched Joe with some interest because he took an egg in each hand and cracked them

51

together. That is all right with the first three, but what does one do with the fourth? Hit it on a stone? Or the toe of the boot? No, he cracked it on the edge of the pan, as, according to my upbringing, he should have done the others.

I didn't comment, but he saw I was interested and said, "I had a young fellow camping with me once and he told me I broke eggs the wrong way. 'Joe,' he said, 'youse ought to hit 'em on the edge of the pan, all of 'em. Not just the last one.' Well, sir, I'm a good cook. Cooking's a trade and I learnt it on my grandfather 's farm when I was knee-high to a grass-hopper. Six years old I was, and I did all the cooking —potatoes, turnips, everything. And here was this man as had lived in a city all his life telling me I didn't know how to crack an egg. 'Well, you show me how you'd do it,' I said to him. So he takes an egg and he gives it such a smack on the pan that he cuts it clean in two and half of it falls in the fire. I said, 'That's the way you do it, is it?' "

All of which made me grateful that I had made no comment myself.

Our first breakfast in the bush was one to remember. Three slices of bacon each and two eggs. "You know," said Joe, "there's millions and millions of people in this war as would go down on their knees and thank God for a meal like this. And what do we do? We moans because there is no sauce and we say the bacon's cooked too crisp and the eggs is cracked the wrong way."

We, meaning I, hadn't said anything of the sort, but we let it go.

He seemed determined to make his point, which was that campers didn't appreciate good cooking by the guides. Returning to the attack he said, "They stand around you as if you was going to put dirt in the pan. I said to a camper once, 'Come along and look at me now. I'm just going to put in the poison.' He took the hint, that fellow, and kept away the rest of the trip. But they're not all like that. I was with a big party this year, four men and three guides, and as soon as we started to cook they all come crowding round the fire. Well, sir, we tricked 'em in the end. We guides had a camp fifty yards off in the bush and we did all the cooking there. One of us would light the fire at their camp and make as if to start cooking. He'd boil, maybe, a pail of water for the tea, and they'd all stand round looking. Then I'd come up behind and put the whole meal on the table. 'What youse all looking at the fire for while the lunch is getting cold on the table?' I'd call. 'Sorry, Joe,' they'd say. 'Didn't know you had cooked it. Thought you were just starting.' 'There's a lot of things about the bush youse don't know,' I'd say to them."

When we broke camp after breakfast Joe put a lot more care into the packing than he had done the first morning. All the heavy stuff went into the best pack, the one with the widest shoulder straps. The pack with the strap that the rabbits had gnawed was filled with the lighter, more bulky stuff, such as fry-pans and tea-pails, which Joe called "the machinery."

While we were at work there was a sudden tremendous din and the whole family of shell-ducks came tearing past, churning up the water in their frantic haste to become airborne. I nodded towards them and Joe said, "Yeah, I see 'em. But I'm wondering what frightened 'em." He was one ahead of me there. I thought only of the ducks. I went to the other end of the island and there, on a stump out in the water, was the biggest gull I have ever seen in my life. It was grey, and looked as big as a goose.

In great excitement I went back and described it to Joe. "Arctic gull," he said "There is one around here. We call it the dive-bomber. He'll dive-bomb anything, fish-hawks, cranes, anything. They're all afraid of him."

It was after ten when we got away and ten-thirty by the time we reached the start of the portage at the lake. Some of the boys had already left and the others were packing up and starting along the track with great ambitious burdens.

This portage was one of the hardest of the trip, but if boys of ten and twelve could make it with one pack, I thought, I should be able to struggle along with two. Joe went ahead with the canoe and I set out to take the two heaviest packs half-way, where I could dump them and return for the rest. The track was very rough as it led through the woods, with steep slopes and tricky patches of broken rock. All along it there were little boys, resting by their packs. Once they had been dropped the packs were too heavy to lift back, and the boys had to wait for someone to come along to give them a heave. I helped half a dozen get going again and each time I did so the second of the two packs I was carrying fell off. I was trying to count my paces, so that I could judge the half-way mark, a quarter of a mile from the start. But every time I stopped to help one of the boys I lost count and in the end went nearly the whole way. If I hadn't met Joe coming back I might have gone right through to the next lake.

On the return journey I found most of the boys I had

helped were sitting down again. There was one who had gone only 10 yards since I left him. "Come, come," I said. "You'll have to do better than that. What sort of a man will you grow into if you don't try?"

With lowered eyes and bottom lip stuck out he muttered: "I don't care. I don't want to be a man."

He was still there when I came back with my second load, his rebellious lip sticking out even further than before.

At the finishing end of the portage the boys who had made it were resting in the shade and I dumped my load and sat down, too. One of them came over and asked if I was a guide. Stroking my chin, with its two-day growth of beard, I shook my head and pointed to Joe. "He's the guide," I said. "He's an Indian. I'm just the man who pays."

"Oh," said the boy with disappointment. "We thought you were both Indians."

In other times and in other places I might rather resent being taken for an Indian. But now I felt my stature increase.

I described the boy down the track and asked his name.

"Would it be Porky?" he said. "Or it might be Stinker."

I agreed Stinker was a likely name for him and asked what would happen to him if he wouldn't go on.

"Oh," said the boy airily, "One of the councillors will take his pack. They are responsible for us. I took half the things out of my pack and left them by the track. One of the councillors will bring them along."

"And what," I asked sternly, "is *your* name?"

55

In a chorus the other boys shouted, "Ratface, silly old Ratface."

"You ought to have had the job I had once," said Joe, putting down his load and addressing the boys. "Packing stores to a mining camp in the north. Every man had to be able to carry a 200-pound load—that's more than his own weight. No shoulder straps either, just head straps. At the end of the season my neck was so stiff I couldn't turn my head for weeks."

The boys did not seem very interested. If Joe had told them something about hunting or scalping they might have listened more attentively, but hard work was something that had not yet entered into their philosophy.

Joe launched the canoe and piled in the packs. The water was shallow at the edge of the lake and on the bottom, lying across the stones and waterlogged timber, was ten feet of chain with rusting three-inch links. Joe pointed it out to one of the boys and said, "Looks as if Paul Bunyan's dropped his watch-chain." The blank, uncomprehending stare that met this sally showed that the North American boy is not always well up in his local folk lore.

"That's not his watch-chain," I said. "That's the bit that goes between his cuff-links."

Now I'm not well up in American folk lore either. But only a few days before I had read an article that was mostly about Paul Bunyan, so I knew he wasn't the author of *Pilgrim's Progress*. Had I been quicker off the mark, I would have made Joe sit down, then and there, and tell us all he knew about the mighty man of the woods. Such a redoubtable story-teller as Joe might have added something new to Bunyan lore.

56

But I missed my chance, so I will quote you from *Life* magazine.

"The real Paul Bunyan," says *Life,* in a copy I stole from a Washington dentist's waiting-room, "was a French-Canadian logger who was in the Papineau Rebellion against Queen Victoria in 1837. The biggest story told about him in Canada was that he could carry 500 pounds over a ten-mile portage. Some time before 1860, U.S. lumberjacks heard about him and adopted him as their greatest hero. They said Babe, his wonderful blue ox, was born in the Winter of the Blue Snow, and in the same year Paul came down across the border to cut logs in the U. S.

"Paul Bunyan was the strongest man who ever lived. One time he was challenged to a fight by Hels Helsen, his big Swedish foreman. They fought all over the Dakotas, on top of a mountain that stood on its head. When they were through, there was nothing left of the mountain but a few blood-darkened humps of earth which are now the Black Hills. They rolled around so much they knocked down all the trees in the Dakotas and left nothing but bare prairie-land.

"Paul had a book-keeper named Johnny Inkslinger, who used two dozen ink barrels at a time with a hose line attached to each one. His cook, Pea Soup Shorty, fed the men nothing but pea soup. In cold weather he froze the soup around a rope and sent it out to the woods in big candles. Paul himself invented many things including the double-headed axe, picture post-cards and poker. When Kansas was covered with whisky trees and everybody there was getting drunk Paul set Babe to logging off the trees so that his men would work better, and Kansas has been dry ever since.

"On a trip to the West Coast for Babe's health,

57

Paul built Pike's Peak, painted the Grand Canyon, and pulled out a row of big stumps to form the Yosemite Valley. He kicked a chunk of land away from the Oregon coastline to make a whale corral and this became Coos Bay. The only thing that ever really baffled Paul was woman. The first time he saw one, he picked her up in his hand for a while, then set her down and walked off sadly into the northern woods. But one legend claims that he really had a wife of his own, with a skin as white and delicate as wood pith from a newly sawn log, and that he used to disappear occasionally into the woods to be with her.

"Paul Bunyan flourished all over the West until the Spring the Rain Came up from China, when it rained upward through the ground for 40 days and nights. This washed away all the wild Western logging country and Paul vanished into U. S. legend."

That's Paul Bunyan for you. There are other stories I have read that credit him with making the flat world round, so that Columbus could discover America, and with putting in the North and South Poles, but personally, I don't believe them.

The lake we were now on was called Little Otterslide. Otters, as you may know, knew about "Strength Through Joy" long before Hitler, and one of their ways of becoming joyful is to slide down steep banks on their tummies and fall into the water with a splash—mother, father, and the children, one after the other. The otter slide that gave this lake its name was close to a little creek that joined it to Otterslide Lake proper. There was a five-foot drop from the bank into the water. But no otters. They are shy, and although we had left behind us nine canoe-loads of boys three others had gone this way just ahead of us. If there were any otters around, they had gone into hiding by the time we arrived. Along this creek we came across our first beaver dam and lodge. But no beavers.

The lodge was rather a disappointment, for it looked nothing more than a pile of sticks about three feet high and without shape or form. In all the pictures of beaver lodges that I have seen, they are shown as neatly rounded at the top, like the dome of St. Paul's. I made a formal complaint about this to Joe. He said they weren't all as bad as this. Some "were as round as a bees' house." The dam was not up to specification either. The illustrations I had seen looked like the Great Boulder Dam on a reduced scale, but this was a puny affair which didn't raise the water more than an inch or two. The top was made of small sticks and we had little difficulty sliding over it in the canoe.

Joe said it was a new dam made in place of one that had been broken by a storm. In a year or two, if the beavers were left alone, they would build it up until the water level rose a couple of feet or more. On both banks were signs that the builders were still on the job; saplings and small trees felled and in the process of being cut into proper lengths, stones for strengthening the foundations and bushes still green, ready for stuffing up cracks.

While we were negotiating the dam, a frog took a high dive from a rock ten feet above the water and fell with a plonk in the river.

"See that?" I said to Joe, rather pleased with myself for having caught it with my eye while still in mid-air.

"Yes, I saw it," said Joe. "I saw the snake, too."

"The snake?"

"Yeah, the snake that was chasing it. Youse don't think a frog would jump like that if something wasn't after it. It was a snake. I saw him in the grass before the frog jumped."

I remembered the ducks and the gull that had frightened them. How much I must have missed already, and how much more I was going to miss before the trip was over.

I said to Joe, "Next time you see a snake chasing a frog, or anything living at all, point it out to me. That's what I've come to see."

Joe shrugged his shoulders. What could you do with a man who couldn't read the book of nature when it was spread out in front of him? Who saw ducks take off in alarm and didn't ask himself what had frightened them? Who watched frogs jump from a ten-foot rock and didn't look for the cause? He knew too much about city folks to think you could ever teach them to use their eyes and their heads. The best you could do was try to please.

We hadn't gone more than a few yards farther down the river when Joe stopped paddling and whispered, "H'st, it was just round this bend we see a moose last time I came through."

We let the current take us, so that we should make no noise with our paddles. Round the corner the river widened into a swamp, and Joe seemed almost trembling with excitement as he whispered, "There he is."

The predominant colour of the swamp was green, but across the far side there was a patch of formless brown that I supposed was the moose. It was quite motionless, and as we drifted down, with only our heads showing above the reeds, the patch of colour grew head and then horns. We passed abreast of it, perhaps two hundred yards away, and still it didn't move. In another minute we would drift out of sight. It was then that my head, if not my eyes, saved me from making a fool of myself. I raised my paddle and brought it down with a smack that should have startled every living thing within half a mile. The "moose" didn't move. In fact, it hadn't moved for 50 years, for I could see now that it was nothing more than a tree stump.

"You'll have to find a better moose than that before you get the boots promised you," I said.

Quite shamelessly, Joe answered, "Well, sir, you'd be surprised at how many people I have taken through here and think to this day they've seen a moose. It pleases 'em and it don't harm no one."

"You'd have had me, Joe," I said, "if it hadn't been for those three canoe loads of boys ahead of us. I just couldn't see any moose hanging around after they passed by."

If you have read the same books that I have, you will remember the correct way to find a moose is to blow on a horn made of birch bark. The moose thinks he hears a lonesome female calling and comes crashing through the bush to make a date. I asked Joe if he could not produce a moose for me in this way. But he shook his head and said it was the wrong time of year.

"The breeding season is the time to do those tricks." he said.

"It really does work, then?"

"Yes, it works all right, especially if you has a pail of water handy," he said. "You see, sir, that old bull moose, he's not such a fool as you might think. First of all, he hears the call and gets so excited, he drops whatever he's doing and comes rushing through the brush, all worked up. Then he gets a bit nearer, and stops to think it over. 'Maybe she's not so good-looking, after all,' he says to himself. 'And even if she is, it wouldn't do to go rushing in on her just like a wild animal.' That's when you has to blow the horn very coy, to make him think he's really going to get something good. He comes a bit nearer but stops again and says, 'That's a mighty queer voice she's got on her. Maybe she's not worth troubling over.' He's just like a young man at the street corner, you see. He can't make up his mind whether the girl is worth following or not. What do you do when you finds yourself in a position like that? Why, you stands in a doorway till she comes by, and you can get a good look. Well, sir, that's just what the old moose does. He says to himself, 'I'll just hang around a bit and see this old cow go by before I commits myself.'

"That's not a bit of use to the hunter. He can't see the moose because of the brush. He can make a noise like a cow, but he can't ever look like one, however he tries. No, sir, the hunter has to think of something else to make the moose come out of the brush. That's why he has the pail of water. He tips it up and empties it slowly so the water splashes on the rocks and makes a noise just like it was a cow doing something. That bull moose is a rude fellow and don't like to miss anything that may be good, and he comes rushing out of the brush into the open to see what goes on and that's when you shoots him."

"A somewhat dirty trick, I should say."

"Well, sir, it's how you looks at it. When people does things like that, it's called 'dirty,' but when animals does them it's called 'natural.' "

We crossed the main Otterslide Lake and came to the next portage at an old ruined lumber camp where, Joe said, he once worked as a cook. The man who made the camp had very hard luck. He built a sawmill by the railroad, then spent the winter cutting logs on Otterslide, ready to take down when the ice thawed. One night the sawmill burnt down, and after paying the loggers' wage bill, he hadn't the money to build another one. So the logs lay around and rotted.

There were hundreds of them there now, 30 or 40 years after, some still floating, others waterlogged and covered by mud.

The portage was only 11 chains long, a rather muddy little path lined with wild raspberry canes. After getting our loads over, we picked the fruit in handfuls and sat in the shade eating it.

"That party with the outboard must have camped on Otterslide last night," said Joe.

"How do you know that?"

"See that track there," he said, pointing to a footprint in the mud. "Made this morning, that was,"

There were scores of tracks in the mud, and all of them looked to me as if they might have been made that morning.

"How do you know it's one of that party?" I asked. "It might have been one of the councillors."

"No," said Joe. "That's not one of the councillors. That was made by the man who carried the motor down the bank to the canoe. He had very big feet that man. I looked at 'em specially. And I know that kind of boot. It's American, and all the councillors is Canadian boys. Yes sir, I saw that man's feet and I'd know his track anywhere."

63

This last portage had brought us to the creek which joins Otterslide with Big Trout Lake. It is about three miles long and has six portages. We reached it at one o'clock and didn't get through till five in the afternoon.

The first stretch of navigable water was no more than a quarter of a mile long and then the creek was blocked by rocks and boulders, the size of houses. Another short portage and we embarked again, paddling between low islands of grey bush through which the creek wound in tortuous half-circles and right-angle bends. An extra two feet of water would have transformed the surroundings into a lake over which we could have taken the canoe anywhere instead of having to follow the winding course we were now forced to take.

"Last time I was here," said Joe, "I paddled straight across the muskeg."

The muskeg! To my English ears the word just breathed adventure. In boyhood I knew it as well as any in the language. I read it a score of times in those hours with Jack London in the hay loft and during illicit candle-light sessions in bed. Now, for the first time in my life, I heard it actually spoken, and spoken in casual, passing conversation, as if it was cheese or a pair of boots, something I was supposed to know all about. And, of course, I did know all about it—everything except what it meant. You didn't have to know its meaning in the days when I came across it in my reading, for it was an atmosphere word like billabong and pinyon, carrying its own message without need of further explanation. Now, I thought it time to make further inquiries.

Joe waved his hand in a lordly gesture, taking in everything in sight.

"Do you mean that's muskeg?" I said, pointing to the nearest bush, something like a lavender.

"That's right," he answered.

"But Joe," I said, "you told me only an hour ago that that was a Labrador bush."

"So it is."

"Well, then, what's muskeg?"

"That is," he said, and this time pointed to an entirely different plant that he had previously named beaver bush.

"I don't get this," I said. "Do you mean that Labrador bush and beaver bush are both muskeg?"

"Course they're not," he said. "Why'd they have those names if they was something else?"

"Well, then, we're back where we started. What (pause) is (pause) muskeg?"

"This is muskeg," he said. "This and this and this. It's a word they use, that's all. They talks about 'walking through the muskeg,' but just which Jeezly bit it is I don't know. I guess that the bush itself is Labrador bush, but the moss and stuff round the roots is muskeg."

I thought at the time this was a poor explanation. I was disappointed in Joe. But I find, on consulting the dictionaries that he didn't do so badly. The Shorter Oxford Dictionary—the two-volume affair —doesn't give the word at all. The two-volume Webster says it is "a sphagnum bog, especially with tussocks in it," and gives its origin as Algonquin Indian. The 12-volume Oxford Dictionary gives quotations from half a dozen writers, and all of them used the word differently.

I might have continued to question Joe on the matter of muskeg if something more important had not happened. He suddenly whispered, "There's a beaver."

It was coming round the next bend in the stream, about 25 yards away and swimming towards us, a brown furry head with nose lifted high. We stopped paddling and sat motionless. The beaver came on at a great pace, until I could see its black little eyes glistening in the fur. Still it didn't deviate from its course. It was only ten feet from the canoe, five feet, I could have almost touched it with my paddle, and it was still swimming. Then it saw us. The water around it swirled. Out came its head and shoulders. I could see the claws of its forefeet, and water dripping from saturated fur. Then down went the head and up came a gigantic brown rump that seemed out of all proportion to the front end. The great flat tail, just as it looked in the picture books, rose until it was vertical in the air, then tail, back legs and rump crashed down on the water together and bubbled from sight.

The splash was made deliberately, to warn other beavers, but I don't think I have ever seen a wild creature perform a less graceful manœuvre.

Joe looked at the widening circle of ripples and said, "Well, sir, that's a beaver."

CHAPTER V

THERE were other beavers to come, but none gave such a thrill as this first one. He, alone, repaid the effort of coming north. Some people shoot wild animals, others photograph them. I find I can satisfy the collector's urge by seeing them in their native state and filing them in my memory. I must confess I have not always thought along these lines. As a boy I lived in the country outside London and shot rabbits and weasels with a .22 rifle. I skinned them, and, after drying the pelts with alum, nailed them to the wall of my room. At night I slept surrounded by my trophies and pretended to be a trapper in his log cabin. My sisters used to say that if I had to pretend to be a trapper, why couldn't I just pretend to kill the rabbits? I didn't see it that way at the time.

Joe said the reason our beaver came so close to the canoe was because the wind blew our scent behind us and not ahead.

"The old beaver don't see well," he said. "He has about the worst eyes in the bush, that fellow. I reckon he was sitting up on the bank somewhere and heard us talking, so he took to the water, where he feels safe."

"What would he be doing on the bank? Working?" I asked.

"No." said Joe. "I reckon he just found it too hot indoors. Those beavers houses gets mighty warm in summer, and smell too. What would you do if you lived in a beaver house in this heat? You'd get out of it, of course, and find a nice cool bank by a stream with a bit of shade to it, and that's what he was doing."

We were now getting into real beaver country and passed half a dozen lodges in as many minutes. Some were out in the open water and those seemed to be the ones that were best constructed. Others were little more than large piles of sticks against the bank. Very slum-like, I thought, with no look of pride about them.

67

At frequent intervals along the bank we saw smears of mud, mixed with twigs evidently dragged from the bottom of the water. Joe said they were the beavers' castoring-places. This was new to me. I thought castor was an oil or a thing you put under the leg of a bed. So I asked what went on at these castoring places, thinking that perhaps beavers suffered from bowel trouble and had to take something for it.

"Well," said Joe, "these are the places they leave their castor, that's all."

"Yes, but what *is* their castor? And why should they want to leave it anywhere? Can't they keep it at home, in a bottle or something?"

Joe put on that air of resigned patience he reserved for my more stupid inquiries.

"It's this way," he said. "The beaver don't need a bottle. He has the castor inside him all the time. All of them have it, the he's and the she's. It's like a sort of juice, and there's special parts they have just under the tail to make it. Now, if a beaver is going some place and he wants the other beavers to know where it is, he makes one of these castoring places. Then he takes a stick and rubs it on his behind until there's some castor on it. After that any other beaver can come along, smell the stick and know where the first fellow's gone, upstream, downstream or where."

"You mean they write messages to each other by rubbing sticks on their bottoms?" I asked in astonishment.

"That's about how it is," said Joe. "Say there's a beaver wants a mate very bad. He's tired of being alone, and wants to take a wife, and he doesn't see just what he fancies around. What does he do? What would you do?"

68

"Well, I certainly wouldn't rub my bottom with a stick."

"Perhaps you wouldn't" said Joe, "but you'd advertise, wouldn't you? You'd write maybe to some friends and ask if they knows of a nice little girl not doing anything just now. One going about a hundred pounds stripped, perhaps, and you'd send your picture, so they could show it to any girl they heard of. Well, sir, that's what the beaver does. Only he don't have no schooling, he don't carry no big fountain pen around with him, so he says what he wants with his castor. And I reckon it's pretty smart to be able to do that."

Joe paddled to the bank beside one of these castoring places, and, pulling out a stick from the mud, smelt it as a connoisseur would a cigar.

"Long time since that beaver was here," he said, handing the stick over to me. I put it to my nose. It smelt just like any other muddy stick dragged from the bottom of a stream. I could detect no hidden meaning whatever. In the R.A.F. they teach you how to decipher visual and oral messages only. I never did learn to decode smells.

We let the canoe drift until we came to another castoring-place, and Joe again pulled a stick from the mud, and after a sniff, threw it to the ground with an exclamation of disgust.

"By the Jove," he said, "that beaver wants a mate bad. He's so lonely he'd take on a widow with a wooden leg."

Curiosity overcoming distaste, I took the stick Joe had thrown down and tried it myself, but found no such Rabelaisian suggestion. It was just like the other stick to me, only perhaps a little smellier.

69

"How do you know," I said to Joe, "that this is a male beaver's message? Perhaps it's the wooden-legged widow advertising."

Joe had to admit there might be some truth in this. He could not himself distinguish the difference between the castor of gentleman and lady beavers. But they knew themselves, he said.

Since getting home, I have read books about beavers, and though all of them mention the castor, none of them say what it is for. Several report that it once fetched a very high price, and was used medicinally, but just what it cured they do not say.

A naturalist I have consulted said that beavers probably can tell the difference between male and female castor, and in the breeding season it may have a different smell to other times. He didn't believe they could indicate with it which way they had gone. Joe, however, was very definite on this point. He said he had watched a beaver go up to a castoring-place, take a sniff and immediately head upstream. Then another had come along, smelled around, and gone upstream too. Then a third and fourth did exactly the same thing. From that he concluded the castor had been put there in the first place by a beaver who wanted to let his pals know where to find him.

Nothing could surprise me about beavers after this. When we came to a large pool, with a dam at one end, Joe pointed to a beaver lodge close by and said it was where the dam-keeper lived. "He has his house near the dam," he said, "so he can look after it. The other beavers gets his food for him and leaves it at his house every day. He's too busy working on

70

the dam, keeping it in repair, to have time to get brush for himself."

Possibly I would have written to the Zoo to ask if this was true, too, had not Joe, grinning like a guilty schoolboy, said, "That's not right really. I just made it up."

This was the only incident of its kind on the trip, the only time Joe openly confessed he was leg-pulling. I had taken his bait, hook, line and sinker, but with no third party present to laugh at his wit he had to confess in order to reveal it. There may have been other times when he deliberately pulled my leg without admitting it but somehow I doubt it, for he liked his own jokes too much to keep them long to himself.

Harmless jokes on campers were his delight. He almost persuaded one man to believe in the Little Men of the Woods. Every night before going to sleep this man wanted to clean out the frying-pan, and every night Joe said, "No, leave it by the fire and it will be clean in the morning." When they got up for breakfast the pan was always spotless. One night the man waited up to observe the Little Men for himself. He was rewarded by seeing some rabbits hop out from the bush and start licking the pan.

"That man was so pleased, he woke me up to tell me; he said, 'Hey, Joe! Those fellows that cleans out your frying-pan are here and they want to speak to you.'"

Another time a fox dug a hole under the wall of the tent and stole a trout that was being saved for breakfast. Next night Joe's client said no fox was going to steal his fish this time and wrapped it in paper and took it to bed with him. Joe rose early

71

and removed the fish by stealth. He filleted it, wrapped the bones and insides up in the paper and replaced the parcel in the man's bed.

"You never saw anyone so 'perspexed' in your life," said Joe. "He unwrapped the parcel to get the fish and there was only bones and guts left. 'Well, by the Holy Moses, that fox has been having breakfast in bed with me,' he said."

The beaver dam that Joe and I were approaching was the finest we saw. It was built between two rocks on either side of the stream and was so wide at the top that you could walk across it dry-foot. The rocks were forty feet apart and the whole structure must have been ten feet thick at the base. It raised the water level by at least four feet and looked as if it had been there for years, decades perhaps. The ends had filled up with soil from which grew grass and saplings. Some master-beaver-mind had chosen the site, just where the rocky sides of the stream almost joined each other. Above, the flooding had formed a deep, wide lagoon and below was nothing but a trickle of water rnuning between miniature canyon walls.

This dam-building seems to be an urge with beavers, for apart from the dams that do some good we saw many that were quite useless. They build them to raise the water level around their houses, which are considered unfit for habitation if the front door isn't under water. But many of the dams we came across achieved nothing, for they were built above or below perfectly good existing dams. Perhaps there is a beaver motto that "idle teeth make idle minds" and when there is no necessary work on hand they just create it, to keep themselves out of mischief. Maybe the type of beaver who is content with the dam his fore-fathers built never learns to work himself and spends his time riotously writing rude messages with his castor.

Later on Joe and I found one place where a beaver lived alone. To improve his morale he had started to build a dam across a lake two miles wide. Every storm destroyed his puny efforts and the beach was littered with relics of his futility. But who knows what temptations of the flesh that beaver was able to resist? What purity of the mind he achieved through his patience and perseverance? When his Maker calls on him to rest, when he has bitten his last tree, and gnawed his final log, he will arrive at the Pearly Gates with a free conscience and a happy mind, be-lieving he has lived a beautiful and blameless life. There are people like that.

The scientific explanation of why a beaver must keep up his gnawing is that otherwise his front teeth would grow so long that he couldn't shut his mouth or eat.

Joe said a beaver lives for 14 years, if it isn't killed by trappers or wolverines. They have reached the age of ten in the London Zoo and a case is on record of a beaver that was 19 years old. There are seven mem-bers of a healthy family—the two parents, four kittens and one young one kept on from the previous year to help with the housework. Until he is three a beaver is free to drop in on his parents any time he wishes. After that he goes off and founds a family of his own.

In the Algonquin Park the beavers, like all other wild creatures, except fish and wolves, are protected all the year round. That is why there are so many there. In other parts of the province a trapper may kill up to 10 beavers in a season. A good quality skin is worth about 50 dollars, so it is a profitable business. Many trappers kill far more than the permitted ten. They sell the extra ones in the black market. Joe says this is a very highly organised racket and most illicit furs are sent to the cities by aeroplane. So are furs trapped out of season, another thriving business.

If you should want a beaver for yourself they can be tamed. I have an old natural history book, written about a hundred years ago by a man called Captain Thomas Brown, F.L.S., M.W.K. and P.S. (whatever that may mean), which has several stories of people who kept beavers as pets. One, owned by a Mr. Broderip of London, built dams in the drawing-room. It laid the foundation with broom handles and a bed-warming pan, then carried on with hand brushes, rush baskets, boots, books, sticks, cloths and dried turf. The smaller gaps were filled up with coal and hay. Having built its dam from one wall to the other the beaver stood back a little to judge its handiwork and, if satisfied, proceeded to comb its hair with the nails of its hind feet, ". . . an operation," says Mr. Broderip, "that showed a beautiful adaptation to the necessities of the animal." I don't know what Mrs. B thought of these goings-on in her drawing-room.

Should you still want a beaver for yourself after reading this I will tell you how to catch it. First you find a beaver house. Then you put a net over the front door. After that you simply pull the house down, stick by stick, until you reach the bedroom, by which time the beavers will have rushed out and got caught in the net. Another method is to make several holes in the ice before pulling down the house. After staying under water as long as they can the beavers put their heads through the holes to take breath and you grab them.

Nowadays most people use steel traps. There are two kinds, depending on whether you want your beaver alive or dead. Joe said he used an ordinary steel spring trap, size No. 4 with jaws that open to a diameter of about six inches. He set this four inches under water and attached a stone weighing about four pounds. He used no bait, but as a refinement sometimes made an artificial costoring-place near the trap, using castor from a previous kill. He took no special precautions, as with other animals, to disguise the human smell. The idea of the stone was to drown the beaver.

"If he don't get drownded quick he'll chaw through his leg in the trap just like it was wood. Then all you finds when you comes along is a beaver foot in your trap," Joe told me.

The other kind of trap is for catching beavers alive. There's a good deal of this done in Canada now. Park rangers and game wardens do it to restock depleted areas and some of the more far-sighted trappers have found that it sometimes pays them to do it too. The trap is built of chain mesh, something like the old chain mail, except that the meshes are two or three inches across. The mesh is fitted into a steel frame and when closed it is much the same shape as a gladstone bag. When open the whole thing lies flat and is placed on a beaver runway near the water with a bunch of freshly cut alder, poplar or birch twigs just beyond. The beaver comes ashore, sees the twigs and comes back. He steps on the spring of the trap, there is a loud rattle of chains and there he is, neatly packed in the gladstone bag ready for taking away.

With all this information you should have no diffi-

75

culty in catching your beaver if you live in North America. In England it wouldn't be so easy. But it might be worth while trying the Vale of Health ponds on Hampstead Heath. A fisherman threw in his line there once and pulled out a baby seal. The theory was advanced at the time that it was illegitimate and had been abandoned by its mother because it interfered with her stage career, and if a foundling seal, why not an unwanted beaver? It does not seem any less likely.

I wanted to ask Joe more about beavers, whether they were happy in their work, if they ever had tooth-ache and other questions that occurred, but he was getting hungry. And when Joe was hungry it was best to let questions wait. The time was two o'clock and we had been working hard on the portages. The big dam made another portage necessary and he said we would have lunch before making it.

We lit a fire on the only open patch of ground near the dam, and sat, waiting for the water to boil, on the trunk of a silver birch newly felled by the beavers. It was a foot in diameter and had been felled with such skill that the top end had fallen in the water alongside the dam. Many of the branches had already been gnawed off and used for repairing weak spots. Eventually the whole tree would be chewed into lengths and used.

While we were eating, the boys we had overtaken earlier in the day came up. Stinker and Ratface were looking very dejected. This canoeing business wasn't working out as they had expected. There was too much hard work about it.

Stinker said to the councillor in his canoe. "Look, they have stopped for lunch, can't we?" "No," said

76

the councillor, "you can't. You can have something to eat when you've carried your pack over this next portage." Stinker looked at us and began to whine. "Don't you think it is time we should eat?" he said to Joe.

Joe grinned and said, "Well, I'm hungry, anyway."

"There you are," Stinker wailed. "The guide says it's time to eat, and he ought to know 'cos he's an Indian."

The councillor, his authority threatened, ordered them on.

When we moved on ourselves we found the track littered with little boys flopped down beside their packs. Stinker had gone no more than a few yards before giving up. Ratface hadn't done much better. Both of them were crying. There were two more portages before reaching Big Trout Lake and the councillors had my sympathy. They were not only carrying the canoes and most of the luggage, but it looked as if they would soon have to carry the boys as well.

After our final portage the river joined the lake in a long muddy estuary. There was so little water that the canoe wouldn't float with Joe and me and our gear on board. I had to get out and walk along the mudbanks while Joe, using the paddle as a punt pole, pushed his way laboriously through the reed beds. A mile ahead the open water of the lake sparkled in the sun, mocking us as we sweated in the mud. Several times Joe had to get out and the two of us pushed the canoe over specially bad patches. The heat was intense and the mud and rotten vegetation stank to high heaven.

Joe said it was all right for me because I came from Washington, which was a hot place, but he didn't like the heat and had never been the same man since getting sunstroke a few years back.

"Until then," he said "I looked no more than 20. But that sunstroke laid me out for two years. Put me on my back and I couldn't work. No man should be asked to live in a climate he isn't reared in. What happened to those two Eskimos they brought down to Montreal? They kept them in a refreezerator, but they died. Thought they'd get used to the climate gradually, but it wasn't natural. They couldn't stand it. They just sweated to death."

As the estuary neared the lake we came to a beaver colony with half a dozen lodges close together. Joe had told me about this place and said we would come here one evening while we were camping on the lake and watch the beavers at work. But it was quite clear there were no beavers there now, for the water had shrunk away from their lodges and left them almost high and dry, like great piles of bleaching bones. There was nowhere between the colony and the lake where they could build a dam, so the village would remain deserted until the autumn rains raised the level of the lake.

When the water was deep enough, I got back into the canoe and together we paddled out into the lake. Joe said there was a camping site just round the corner that was the best in the Park. He had spent a week there earlier this season and built two tables fit for a king. But when it came in sight we saw the three canoes that had been ahead of us all day were pulled up on the rocks and the boys were already erectiny tents. To Joe this was the last straw after a hot and tiring day. He had been thinking of that camp site with its beautiful tables ever since I first suggested

78

going to Big Trout Lake. It was a prize, a promised reward for the sweat and toil of the portages we had just come through, and now it had been snatched from under his nose.

He was so dispirited that he just sat hunched on his seat, with the paddle across his knee. I couldn't share his misery, for the site did not look specially attractive to me. A couple of miles ahead lay a large wooded island that seemed to promise much more interesting camping. Joe said there was a site on the island and he supposed we would have to go there, but he wasn't cheered by the thought. He lit a cigarette and let the canoe drift on the lake. I was for getting on and making a cup of tea. Joe, the North American, said he'd rather have iced water.

I dipped my hand in the lake and found it almost tepid.

"No good drinking that," said Joe. "If only I had my iced water rig with me I'd give you a drink you'd never forget."

"And what," I asked, "is an iced water rig?"

"Well, sir, I have a water bottle at home that's made of aluminum, the same as an airplane is, and I melted some lead and poured it in the bottom; then I fixed two lengths of line, about 40 feet each, on it. One line I tied on the bottle and the other on the stopper and that's my iced water rig. I lets it down in the lake till the line's all gone, then I give a little jerk on the one that's tied to the stopper and out it comes and the bottle fills with cold water from the bottom of the lake.

"I was out fishing with a woman and her husband once and she says, 'Joe, I'd give five dollars for a drink of iced water.' I had the rig with me in my pack and so I says to her, 'For five dollars I'll get it for you.'

'How you going to do that?' she asks. 'Never mind,' I says to her. 'I'll do it, and then you tell me if it's not the best drink of cold water you ever had in your life.' Well, sir, I let the rig down and pulled out the cork and when it came up the water was so cold there was frost on the bottle."

"Did you get your five dollars?" I asked.

" 'Well,' the woman said, 'Joe, that's the most marvellous thing I've ever seen. It's worth five dollars to know about.' But I said she didn't have to pay, I was only joking. 'No,' said her husband. 'A bargain's a bargain and she'll have to pay you, Joe.' No sooner did her husband say this than just like a woman she did the opposite thing and said of course it was only a joke and she wouldn't pay."

"That was a bit tough on you, wasn't it?"

"No," said Joe. "I know women. I just let her be and at the end of the trip I said to her on the quiet, 'You certainly can handle your husband.' She laughs and adds 10 dollars to my tip. Then the man, he takes me aside and says, 'I'm sorry about my wife and that five dollars, but here's 10 to make up for your disappointment.' "

The memory of this little transaction put new spirit into Joe and he was full of good humour as we took our paddles again and made for the island ahead.

CHAPTER VI

THE camp site on this island was a lot cleaner than the last one at which we stayed. Joe surveyed it with his expert eye and said this was because there had been no boys camping there, only parties with guides. Then he started a systematic search to see what had been left behind. This was routine with Joe at every camp site. Campers are so careless. Soap, salt and toilet rolls were the most common things people leave around. In the eight days we spent in the Park we could have collected a couple of pounds of soap. I suppose people begin these trips with civilised intentions and then, as they get closer to nature, their minds dwell less and less on cleanliness until finally they abandon their soap with their city complexes and go as completely native as one can in a week.

At Big Trout Lake camp I found a fountain pen and two pairs of sun spectacles. Joe found 39 cents and a teaspoon. He reckoned it was a poor haul. We would do better than that before we reached home again, he said. It was a poor trip when he did not find a pocket knife and some useful fishing-tackle.

The camp was on a headland of the island, facing south-east, and gave us a view of half the lake. There was a serviceable table, a cupboard made with a box nailed to a tree and an arm-chair, hacked by some amateur carpenter from a tree stump. Years before a big pine had fallen across the centre of the camp and we had to step over it every time we passed from the tent to the table. The fireplace had been built on a commanding rock at the very point of the island and from it you could see down to rocky beaches on either side. Behind the camp the bush, like a green wall, cut off the rest of the island and the world to the north. In front, the lake was our known friend. We could see it and watch its mood change with the weather and the time of day. The loons and the ducks were our camp-mates, always in sight. But the bush behind was mysterious and unknown. A hundred eyes might be watching us and we would never see them. That wilderness of trees and rotting logs, with the decay of centuries so thick that you sank to your ankle at every step, might be the home of bears, moose and wolves.

We were planning to camp here for three days and in that time it might give up some of its secrets, but in those first few hours after landing I kept glancing back frequently and wondered what went on there.

With three travel-free days ahead we felt we had all the time in the world. For half an hour after searching the camp site we sat in the shade and smoked. Then Joe pulled himself together sufficiently to get a fire going and I took a bathe. As we drank our tea afterwards Joe told me that he had camped on this island once before, with a party of four men. The first evening, while Joe was cooking, they went out fishing and caught more trout than they could have eaten in a week. Joe was disgusted with them, for the rule of the Park is that you don't catch more than you can eat. They couldn't keep the fish, for in the summer heat the lot would have gone bad in a couple of days. But the men said they'd come to fish, and fish they would. "All right," said Joe, "you fish, but I'm going back. I'm not going to lose my guiding licence for a crowd of men who let fish rot on the ground. I have to report every fish you get and how am I going to explain 60 pounds of lake trout taken in one evening?"

In return for a promise not to report them to the rangers, Joe says, he made them eat fish and nothing else three times a day until they were so sick of it they never wanted to see a trout again.

This wasn't a bad case, Joe said. These chaps were just ignorant, "not like the two men and two guides who went to Lake Lavieille the first year it was opened up. They caught so many fish they had to dig a hole four feet by two feet by three feet to bury 'em in. The rangers found their camp the day after they was gone, and followed 'em all the way to the south boundary of the Park, watching everything they did. Those fellows had to pay a huge fine, thousands of dollars, and the guides was never allowed in the Park again."

After listening to talk like this I didn't anticipate much trouble in getting one little fish for supper that night, and five minutes after we launched the canoe and started trolling I had a bite and struck. He was hooked, for I felt the first lunge. Then the heavy copper wire fouled on the reel and I lost a precious second freeing it. When I came to wind in the fish had gone.

"He somersetted," said Joe. "You gave him slack on the line and he got away by somersetting."

We went on trolling, and we went on trolling, and not one fish in Big Trout Lake took the slighest notice of us. We changed from one kind of lure to another and then back again. Joe paddled the canoe for miles and miles in wide sweeping circles and we were completely ignored. When Joe had been telling his stories of gigantic catches I had thought I would set aside

83

the first two fish I caught for ourselves and give the rest to Stinker and Co. In that way I could have a great evening's sport, catch all I wanted and yet know the fish weren't wasted.

But the sun sank lower in the sky, and no fish bit. From the east came the drone of the Park Superintendent's aeroplane returning from the evening fire patrol. "Hear it, howling away?" said Joe. The night breeze came up, rippling the lake with its touch, but still no fish. The cry of the loons began to change from their daytime warble to the eerie notes of night, but no fish struck. When the sun had finally sunk, and the woods were no more than a black margin to the lake, our last sweep took us to the mouth of the creek down which we had come in the afternoon, and there, emerging from the swamp, was a lone canoe. I thought at first it had only one occupant, paddling in the stern, but as it slid past us in the dusk I distinctly saw the huddled forms of Stinker and Ratface asleep in their seats. Close at hand the camp-fires the other boys had lit were twinkling their welcome and promise of rest and succour. But Stinker and Ratface were beyond caring.

I was rapidly getting that way myself and when Joe said it was too dark for the fish to see the bait I was ready to admit defeat for the day.

Joe reckoned it was the weather. He said he thought there was a storm coming and it was well known that fish didn't bit when there was electricity in the air.

"I knew before we started the weather was going to change," he said. "Now everything I see tells me the same thing. That fish we caught yesterday hadn't eaten for days. The electricity put him off his feed."

This was the second time Joe had predicted a

change, but there was still no sign of it. The sky was almost clear of cloud, red where the sun had set and deepening blue above.

As a matter strict scientific fact we were in an area of high pressure and fine weather. I checked this up afterwards with the meteorological maps for the period. It is possible, of course, that the fish and loons knew about a cold front 1,200 miles away, that stretched from Saskatchewan to Wyoming, and was moving slowly in our direction.

As we approached the camp after our unsuccessful fishing expedition the bush behind looked darker and more mysterious than ever. Joe said, "I can hear someone there talking French." A chill of uneasiness went down my spine. I could see no one moving. I could hear nothing. But Joe's ears were so much better than mine that I guessed he had overheard the strangers whispering.

"Who do you think they are?" I said in a whisper myself.

"Don't know," said Joe. "I only know it's French they're talking."

I expected Joe to call out "Who's there?" or something, but he paddled right up to the landing-rock as if nothing had happened. Perhaps he knew they were friends. But why didn't they reveal themselves? Why didn't they come out to meet us? After we had dragged the canoe up the rocks I let Joe go ahead to the camp. He would know what to say to the strangers. No one stepped out from the tent nor from behind a tree, as I had expected. Everything in the camp looked just as it had been, and Joe went to work on the supper without further comment.

It began to dawn on me that there was no one in

the camp at all and that Joe must have been using a figure of speech. I sat down on the big log between the fire and the tent to puzzle it out. It was now quite dark and Joe was cooking a tin of stew by the light of the flames. Around us the usual night sounds had begun—the loon, the ducks and the bullfrogs. The bullfrogs! Of course! They must be the speakers of French.

"Joe," I said, "do bullfrogs ever speak English?"

"No," he answered, without looking up, "only French."

That night round the camp-fire Joe got talking about World War I. They made him a sniper and his best day was when he climbed a factory chimney from the inside and lay on the top. He didn't know how many men he killed, but he was shooting all day. He was getting so many targets that he didn't break off for lunch. It would have wasted too much time. He went on shooting till it was too dark to see, and when he came down he found he'd missed supper and the cook wouldn't give him anything to eat. As a unit in the machine of war Joe had snuffed out a dozen, perhaps 20 human lives that day, but the thing that he remembered 30 years after was missing his lunch and his supper.

"Was that what you got your medal for?" I asked.

"No," said Joe, modestly, "I got that for bravery."

He was out in No Man's Land one night, crouched against a shattered tree stump when he heard a voice right under his feet. Stealthily he worked his way round the stump until his hand touched a metal ring. He felt round and discovered a trap-door. The men under ground went on talking, unaware that in the plains of France they were being stalked by an Algon-

86

quin Indian. Joe pulled the trap-door open and shouted, "Come out, you Jeezly Germans, the war's over." There were 12 of them, says Joe, and he captured the lot. For that they gave him the Military Medal, but he wished afterwards they hadn't because when he came back to Canada they wouldn't let him out of the Army. He had to wait around in Ottawa until the Prince of Wales came and gave him his medal.

I asked how he liked England. He said, "Well, sir, the place I remember best is that building in London where they keep all the artillery and rifles from the Boer War. I spent two days there, looking at all those old weapons. They had spears and swords and poison arrows the Indians made with quills. One touch and you're dead. I guess they never did find out how those Indians got their poison."

I imagine the place Joe spoke of was the Imperial War Museum.

The only complaint he had against London was the "High English" they spoke there. "There's two sorts of English, just as there is French," he said. "There's High English and Broken English. I speak Broken."

Also that night Joe told me about the Indian love root. In the old days, he said, when a brave took a fancy to a girl he threw a stick or a stone on the ground to attract her attention.

"If the girl picks up the stick," said Joe, "the two of them mate up. Well, sir, that's all natural, but there were some Indians didn't get the mates they wanted. The girls wouldn't pick up their sticks, so they began to make up little things like a birch bark bag and decorate them in a way a girl would like, and they threw them on the ground instead of sticks. That would have been all right, but the bad men began

87

to put love root powder in the bags and once she smelled that, a girl would do anything. It's so strong, that
powder, one smell can make a girl run 50 miles in her
bare feet, just to look at a man.

"Well, I was telling this to a young fellow I took
fishing once, and he said, 'Joe, if you get me some of
that stuff I'll give you 200 dollars for it.' I told him
I didn't dare do that. If I was found with love root
in my pocket I'd get into trouble. The Government
doesn't like that root dug up. He thinks it an ugly
thing to do, the Government does. So I told this fellow I couldn't do it for him. 'But,' I said, 'you send
me a handkerchief that you're going to give to the
girl you want, and I'll see what I can do to fix it so
she will take to you.' Well, along comes a handkerchief which must have cost him 50 dollars, all silk
and little pictures. Now there isn't many people know
where this root grows. There's no leaves or plant or
anything to show. You can find places in the bush
where you smell it all round, but unless you know
just where to dig you'll never find it. A full-blooded
Indian showed me the place once and made me promise never to tell. Well, Sir, I went along and I got
some of this root and I dried it in the sun and powdered it up and put it on that handkerchief and sends
it back to the young man. I told him not to give any
money unless it worked. Well, I heard nothing for
several months and then comes a picture of his wedding and 300 dollars with it.

"But that wasn't the end of it. After a couple of
years he comes back for some more fishing and he
comes back alone. I asked him what he done with
his wife. 'I'm divorced,' he said. 'Well,' I told him,
'you better have some more love root and get her back.'

'Holy Jeepers,' he said to me, 'I don't want any more of that stuff. I wouldn't give you a nickel for it now.' "

If anyone thinks a little Indian love root would solve his immediate difficulties I can say that it looks like copper wire, about a sixteenth of an inch thick, and, according to Joe, it drips a red juice like blood when you break it in your fingers. I shall keep my eye open in future when I am digging in the garden. A find of love root in Hampstead might have very interesting results. So should you read in the papers that girls there have suddenly and unaccountably started running about barefoot you will know what's going on.

There was no moonlight bathing on this, the second night of our trip. Joe, as he promised, mixed balsam boughs with the spruce on our bedding, and either that or the long day we'd had sent me to sleep a few minutes after turning in.

In spite of the predictions of Joe, the loons and the fish, the morning dawned fine, with a clear sky and a slight breeze. We were up at seven and on the water at 7.30. After trolling for an hour I caught a five-pound lake trout on a mother-of-pearl spoon, which solved the food problem for that day.

These lake trout are peculiar fish. They have forked tails, which are definitely *démodé* in the best game fish circles of Europe, and there also seems to be a touch of the tarbrush about them somewhere, as if some ancestor had been matey with a pike. The skin is slimy, and there is about the head something not quite thoroughbred trout. I am told that these differences are due entirely to environment and have no connection with the morals of their ancestors.

The trout live their whole lives in the deep-water

lakes, spawning in the gravel. Joe said they drop their spawn in September and October and it lies there until spring, when the male fish works over it again, to make sure it is fertilised. He says he's seen them do it. If this were true it would mean the lake trout had a rather more interesting life than most fish, with two love seasons. Unfortunately it is not true. An official of the Ontario Government whom I consulted says that if any spawn remained unfertilised until spring it would most certainly be dead. The Windermere char has two breeding seasons, but the individuals that spawn in the spring do not do so in the autumn and vice versa.

The other great game fish in this part of the Park is the bass. You sometimes find bass and lake trout living in the same lake, but never in the same part of it, Joe said. Mostly they stick to their own lakes. Both Joe and a man I met in the train coming up from the States told me that one species ate the spawn of the other. I couldn't remember which ate which, so I asked this same Government official and he said neither ate either. They leave each other alone in the spawning season and out of it, he said.

The route that Joe and I were taking on this trip included no first-class bass lakes. Had I known this when I laid my plans I might have done differently, for bass fishing is said to be very fine sport. When I did find out it was too late to change our route, for you are not allowed to wander around these woods just as you like. Yo have to fix your route and stick to it. You go to the Park rangers and tell them exactly where you are going. They then give you a travel permit on which your route is set out. Should you then go somewhere else you have commited an offence under the Forest Fires Prevention Act. This may seem like red tape, but it does enable the rangers to check up in case of fire. There are many fires in the Park each year and nearly all are caused by careless campers. Most of them are put out in a day or two, before they have done much damage, but a really big fire might destroy half the Park for the next hundred years. People like Stinker, Ratface and me would then have to find somewhere else to play at being Indians.

The best month for fishing in these parts is May, Joe said. That is when the fly fishermen come. They are the experts, the purists who will suffer anything for their art, and suffer they do, for flies on the water mean flies on the wing. The moose fly and the deer fly are so big at that time of the year, says Joe, that they cut away chunks of your flesh and fly off with them, to eat at their leisure. The fly fishermen take bottles of insect repellent with them and, at night, light smoky fires at the tent door to discourage the mosquitoes. But if you are a purist the quality of the fishing at this time of year makes it almost worth being eaten alive. The speckled trout that take the fly run to ten pounds and even the lake trout are feeding near the surface in May and are not above an odd fly as hors-d'oeuvre.

Bass fishing starts in July, then tapers off until late August when according to Joe, it is at its best. Other people say it is at its worst then. I didn't try so I don't know. Lake trout slack off in the middle of the summer too but improve as the water gets colder.

There are also pike in the Park, but they are in waters farther north than those Joe and I were travelling. I got to telling Joe about some of the big pike I had caught at home. I told him, truthfully, that one

I saw landed had a duckling in its stomach.

"Well," said Joe. "I caught a pike once, and when I got him on the land it come on to rain, so I opened its mouth and put a stick between the jaws. Then I crawled in till it stopped raining. A darn fine lean-to it made."

After that I didn't tell Joe fishing stories. I just let him tell them to me. His best was about a trout in Burnt Island Lake that pulled the canoe backwards, though Joe was paddling forward as hard as he could. He told me this story several times. At the third telling he said they had an outboard motor in the canoe and put it over the side. Even then, he said the fish still pulled the canoe back. They had to cut the copper line finally because they were being dragged on the rocks.

Joe also told me, several times, the story of Tom Salmon and his 85-foot cast at Brulé Lake. Tom was a maker of snow-shoes. He made them better than anyone else, for he had a special way of drying the rawhide that no one else knew. But when May came along and people weren't wanting snow-shoes he packed up his shop and went fly fishing. One day, standing by the side of Brulé Lake, waiting with other fishermen for the train, he made a bet that he could drop a fly beside a deadhead sticking from the water 85 feet off the shore. Joe took a side-bet with the other spectators that Tom would not only do it, but catch a fish as well. The great cast was made and the fly fell right by the deadhead; there was a mighty swirl and Tom had hooked a fish.

"Of course," said Joe, "I knew he could do it, because I seen him practising on that same deadhead when no one was there. And I knew a fish was feeding there because I saw the water move just before Tom made his bet. He made five dollars out of that cast, and I made 10."

After breakfast I went fishing for minnows. Joe wanted to try them for bait instead of a spoon. He said frogs were the best bait for the minnows.

"What's the matter with bread?" I asked. "Bread's no good," said Joe. "It won't stay on the hook."

Now my ancestors were catching fish in the Thames with bread paste before America was discovered, before anyone had ever heard of the Algonquin Indians. So while Joe was looking for frogs I got to work with the bread to such good effect that I had 14 nice minnows when he returned. I had expected a little praise, or at least an interest in how I had performed the miracle, but Joe's first words when he reappeared were: "Guess what I've just seen round the corner. Two deer, standing in the water among the timber."

"Where?" I asked, minnows and bread paste forgotten.

He described the spot and I set off to see for myself. Of course there were no deer when I got to the place, but there were many signs that they had been there, such as tracks and droppings. This was quite exciting in itself, for the island was not more than a mile long and about the same in width and, if there were deer on it, they could not be far away.

I chose a trail that looked the most recent and set off in search.

CHAPTER VII

THE deer track led over a little blueberry-covered hill and into the woods. Following it was like stepping from the open air into a botanical glasshouse. The trees closed overhead and made a mosaic of the sky. Everything was deathly still. Not a leaf moved, for there wasn't enough air to move it; there was hardly enough to breathe. Every few steps I stopped to look, and listen. In the half-light were a thousand shapes that might have been creatures looking at me. I tried to outstare them, to wear down their patience till they betrayed themselves with a flick of the ear or the tail, but they were rocks or tree stumps, all of them, and did not move. Every dozen yards rotting logs lay across the narrow track, with the moss knocked from the top by the passing feet of animals in a hurry. It was a dead world and no place to dally in the high heat of summer. Fifty feet above there was life, and more lay buried under foot. Up there leaves were sucking in the sunlight and twigs growing. Below a million rootlets were stretching out, feeling for decaying vegetable matter with which to renew the cycle of life. But these were silent processes and at the level of the ground there wasn't so much as a bee to temper the silence with its buzz.

Other trails crossed the one I was following. Some were broad and might have led to more attractive parts of the wood, but there seemed a virtue in following the path I had begun and I resisted their lure. For half an hour I went on like this, and, except for the trees and

94

moss, I didn't see one living thing; not a fly, not an ant, not a bird. Then the trees thinned and opened upon a broad patch of wild raspberry canes. And there was blessed movement in them. Something alive at last was passing through. I stood dead still, fascinated. It couldn't be the deer I had set out to see, for their heads would have shown above the canes. For the same reason it couldn't be a moose. Thirty yards off the movement stopped and the canes were still again. This was more exciting than ever. I dodged behind a tree, hoping to see without being seen. For five minutes I stared at the motionless raspberry canes and nothing happened. Then there was a slight twitch of one leaf—or was there? I couldn't be sure. It twitched again, definitely this time. Then another one moved and another. For one fraction of a second something black, the size of a man's hat, appeared above the canes and was gone again. I didn't see it come up, or go down, but for that fleeting moment of time I looked into the face of a wild bear.

Then the whole raspberry patch was set in motion as the bear moved over the hill and away.

I would rather have that memory in my collection than half a dozen bearskin rugs.

I followed, but I didn't see the bear again, and presently came to the other side of the island. Instead of returning the way I had come I thought I would go back to camp along the rocks at the edge of the lake. It was quite a scramble, for at times the rock rose precipitously from the water's edge to the trees above, and I had to climb round, from one tiny foothold to the next with my tummy pressed flat to the rock, like a lizard. Rounding a bend in this manner I found myself confronted by an enormous bullfrog,

95

as big as a man's fist, sitting on a ledge above the water. It was so near that our faces almost touched. Had I fancied raw frog for lunch I could have opened my mouth and bitten it. The frog looked at me and I looked at the frog. Its expression didn't change, nor the look in its eye. Its only movement was a gulping at the throat. I have never looked a frog in the eyes before, and I tried to detect signs of any recognisable emotions. There were none. I saw neither fear nor surprise in those eyes, neither resentment nor awe. It just sat there and stared and didn't move. Its skin was a darker green and not so shiny as that of our frogs at home. Behind each bulbous eye was a green button, the size of a dime, which Joe said were ears and the scientists call "Tympanic membranes."

It sounds ridiculous, but that frog completely barred my way, as I barred his. Both my hands were fully engaged holding myself on to the rock face and the frog was occupying the next logical handhold. The frog couldn't move back, and if it went forward it would hit me in the face. We were like two cars meeting in a narrow lane. One of us had to give in and, as the frog couldn't, it had to be me. I edged back round the rock and gave a yell to show my retreat was a matter of strategy and not defeat. The frog jumped in the water and I continued my scramble.

It brought me, after strenuous efforts, to a little hollow in the rocks, invisible from the lake and unapproachable from the land except by someone such as myself acting the lizard. It was as perfect a little hide-out as you would ever wish to see, and someone had camped there, and camped recently, for the spruce of the bedding was still green. No tins lay about. There was no mess of any kind. But by the fireplace was a very old hand-carved canoe paddle. This was surely the camp of a real Indian or woodsman.

Hoping to discover some clue to identity I combed through the spruce bedding and was rewarded by finding two scraps of paper. One was a receipt for 10 dollars on Form S. 254 of the Royal Navy and on the other were printed washing directions for Kayser underwear!

I still have the canoe paddle. Joe said it was carved from maple, perhaps 50 years ago, and was certainly the work of an Indian. It is grey with age and the wood is dozey, as though it had been floating for years in the water. Joe thought I was crazy, lugging it around for the rest of the trip. But travellers collect African assegais, Australian boomerangs and Japanese swords, to hang on their walls at home, so what's wrong with returning from Algonquin country with an Indian canoe paddle? Nothing, as far as I can see, yet you should have heard the ribaldry it produced from fellow passengers on the journey home. It was bad enough in the train going back to the States, but the humorists had a field-day when I carried it over my shoulder up the gangway of the *Queen Mary*!

The only other incident before getting back to camp was the discovery of an abominable smell. It came up from between two shoulders and the cause proved to be an animal garbage dump and sewage disposal works. Fishbones were the least unpleasant of the things it contained. Later, I described it to Joe, who said it was made by otters. I like otters. Ever since reading *Tarka* they have had my sympathy. I would like to think that they made this dump in the interests of sanitation, but I fear no such thoughts entered their heads.

97

"Do you know what you done this morning?" said Joe sternly when I reappeared.

"No," I replied, instantly feeling guilty.

"You killed 300 fish."

I thought hard, trying to remember any deed that could possibly have caused such slaughter. Perhaps it was something I had thrown, or deposited, in the water that had polluted the entire lake.

"Yes, sir," Joe continued relentlessly, "you killed 300 fish this morning, and didn't know it. Come and I'll show you."

He led me down to the rock where he had been cleaning our morning-caught trout on a trip of birch bark and pointed to an amber-coloured object six inches long. "Know what that is? That's trouts' eggs," he said, picking it up with a laugh and showing it to me. "That fish you got this morning was about ready to spawn. Just look at the eggs."

The spawn was like orange caviare and there was half a pound of it at least. I asked Joe if it was good to eat.

"It might be all right if you had some place with an oven," he said. "But fish's eggs won't fry. They jumps out of the pan as soon as they hit the fat. They jumps about four feet in the air, those eggs do."

I thought I would experiment that evening and perhaps improve on a four-foot jump, but a blue and white gull swooped down while we were having lunch and flew off with the whole roe.

This fish, like the others, had nothing in its stomach when opened. Joe nodded his head wisely when he pointed this out, and told me to look out at the water on the main body of the lake. The wind had freshened considerably and was whipping the water into little wavelets.

Three miles away, hugging the shore to keep out of the wind and rough water, a cavalcade of canoes was creeping by. Stinker and the boys were on the move. We never did see the party with the outboard motor. They went on to another lake, we were afterwards told.

Joe said it was too rough to fish out in the open water and he was going to spend the morning improving the camp. This, inevitably, meant making a new table. I used the time making short expeditions into the bush and along the shore, returning periodically to ask Joe questions about what I had seen. Working away with his tomahawk and pocket-knife, making a flat-topped table out of two cedar logs, he was in a happy mood and answered as patiently as any parent at the seashore.

I fished some fresh-water clams from the shallows and asked Joe if they were good to eat.

"Some Indians eat them," he said, "but I never done it and don't want to try."

I caught a leech in the water, about four inches long with a black back and a brown belly, and asked if it was good bait. Some people used it for bass, said Joe, but he'd never tried it himself.

I brought him what I called a shrimp and he a crawfish. That made very good bass bait, he said.

Under a bush I found a broken egg-shell. "Grass bird," said Joe, and went on working.

All this rather reminded me of nature walks at school. We were periodically taken into the country by a prim and elderly spinster and were supposed to run about finding things and then bring them back and ask her what they were. Like the beastly little boy I was, I tried to embarrass her once by taking along, on a piece of bark, something I knew perfectly

well had been done by a dog. Without batting an eye-
lid she took the bark in her hand and, at a proper
distance, examined the object closely.

"Let me see," she said, adjusting her spectacles the
better to see with, while we boys held our tummies
to keep from laughing. "Let me see, now. There are
no foxes around here, are there? No, I think it must
be merely dog."

Do you know, not one of us laughed. And ever since
I have regarded these little souvenirs that animals
leave around as a legitimate and proper subject for
nature study. So it was with no wish to embarras Joe,
but in earnest quest for knowledge, that I scraped
something from the top of a rock and took it along.

Without hesitation Joe said, "Mink."

"Now how in the world can you say that with such
certainty?" I asked.

"Well, sir," he answered, "you found that down
there where I was cleaning the fish, didn't you? You
found it on a little rock with a flat top, didn't you?
You don't think I missed a thing like that, do you? No,
sir, trapping animals and knowing all about them is
my living. I have to read the signs like that as you
reads a book. They're my bread and butter.

"And anyhow I know it was a mink because I saw
it. When you was in the bush looking for deer I
had a notion to change my underclothes, so I went in
for a swim. When I was swimming around I saw
that mink come out from the rocks and take a look at
the fish-head lying in the water where I left it. Then
it squatted on the rock and afterwards come in the
water. It come very near, but after it saw me it turned
round and swam back to the shore like all the trappers
in Canada was after it."

For a while I watched Joe making his table. He had cut two lengths from a cedar log, about six inches across, split them down the centre, and was now smoothing off the flat surface with his hatchet. He was fast and deft and I passed some complimentary comment.

"Yes, I'm very good," he agreed, modestly. "Not like these men in the bush to-day who can't score nor hew. In the old days a man cutting timber scored it and squared it on the spot, and it went out squared. To-day you can't get a saw-man or an axe-man to even notch a tree. They can't tell such a simple thing as which way the tree will fall. They're not men to-day, they're women. And eat! Sit 'em down at a table and by Jeepers if there isn't pie or cake they won't work. The old timer didn't have no pie, or no cake, and no sugar neither.

"I was at a camp last year where there was 40 men, and not one of 'em could score or hew. I said to the boss I'd stay along a few days and help him out, as that wood was needed bad for making ships in the war."

"That is very interesting, Joe," I said, " but I'd be more interested if I knew what scoring and hewing was."

"Well, sir, you know what hewing is if you use your eyes, because I'm hewing now at these cedar logs, and scoring, well, that's marking a line down a log where it's to be squared off. You use a scoring axe. It's got an 18-inch blade and can weigh anything up to 15 pounds. They just can't handle an axe like that these days, so I told the boss he must go to an Indian to get a job like that done."

Somewhere there may be a ship on the sea built of

timber that was scored, hewn and squared by our Joe Lavally.

After lunch, when we were sitting back with our mugs of tea and drowsily smoking, Joe told me the story of his brother, who was killed by a Mexican.

"He was shot on his ranch out in the west," said Joe, "and we buried him out there. Didn't want to bring him back because my mother was ill and we feared it would upset her.

"Those people out in that ranch country, they trouble each other a lot, steal cattle and that, and this brother was as bad as any, and I knew it. I went to the jail and saw the lad that shot him and I asked straight out why he done it. I told him to tell me true. 'You don't need to lie to me,' I said, 'I know he was a bad man.' 'Well,' the lad said, 'I shot him because he bothered me.'

"Then the judge ask me what they should do with him. 'You have the best right to say. You're the murdered man's brother.' I said, 'Well, sir, he was an ugly man and you all knows that. You have enough evidence to have killed him several times over, and all this lad done is to finish the job for you and save you the trouble.'

"The judge said, 'Well, Joe, that's true.' So they lets the lad off and I went back with him for a holiday on his farm."

The brother died intestate, and Joe had several letters from a lawyer out west advising him to file a claim for the estate.

"He sent me about 10 letters," Joe said. "In the end I told him he could keep the money. It wasn't mine, I said, my brother left no will and what chance would I have to get it? I told the lawyer I had money of my own without trying to get other people's. Those lawyers are smart. I'd have spent a lot of money and then got nothing because there was no will, see?"

The lawyers may be smart but some of the Algonquin Indians aren't so stupid.

"Who wrote your letters to the lawyer?" I asked.

"My daughter," he said. "She that's a schoolteacher She's a good scholar, reads, writes and everything."

"Don't you ever wish you had learned to read?"

"No," said Joe, "I learned other things that's more useful than reading and writing. I didn't go to school because I had to work on my Indian grandfather's farm, and there was no law then to make me. My grandfather taught me how to cook and build a house, how to pick out the best timber and build a birch bark canoe. He taught me about the animals and how they live and what they eat. I learned useful things on his farm, more useful than they teach you in schools. After the first war there was a big 'compression' in these parts. Nobody could get a job. There's going to be another compression after this war, and then I shall be the big man around here, just you see. Last time, when all these clerks and people was looking for work, I made more money than when there wasn't a compression. I put the whole family, the wife and five children, on to picking blueberries. Then I bought an old truck and took the berries 75 miles into Kingston. Eleven-quart baskets they were, and I took 70 each trip and got two dollars a basket. I tried Toronto, but that was a bad market for berries. They was interested at the beginning of the season but after a day or two they wouldn't look at you. In Kingston I sold all I could get, all through the season.

"My wife was the best picker, she and one son. They

could pick three baskets a day, sometimes four. The others were like me. Not good pickers. If I didn't get a full load of 70 baskets in a week, I could always buy baskets from other people for a dollar fifty. They was only too glad to sell at that price and I made a profit."

"So you reckon education is a bad thing to have when there's a depression on, do you, Joe?"

"Well, sir, I listened once to two men arguing about education. Trustees of a school they were, both of them, and one said the country was going to the devil, and all because of education. 'There's schools, schools, schools everywhere,' he says, 'and what happens? Why, when the compression comes on we have to feed peoples, hundreds of them. They just line up for bread and soup. It's all they're fit for. They're too educated to live. They're no good for anything but sitting at a table with a Jeezly big fountain pen in their hands and a bottle of ink in front. There's not one of them could go out in the bush with an axe and cut down a tree. They couldn't trap a fisher or a mink. All they can do is put a white collar round their necks and count the pencils in their pocket. Why should you and I pay good money to have people educated like that?' he says. 'Why not put them all on a farm when they're six, like Joe here, and make 'em learn something useful? Then we won't have to pay dollars to feed 'em when the next compression comes along.' "

"What had the other fellow got to say, Joe?"

"He was in favour of education. He thought it was a good thing. 'It's a light load to carry,' he says, 'and it weighs nothing. You can take it on a portage and still carry a canoe. It don't take up no room and is a good thing to have with you any place.' "

Joe's sympathies, however, were clearly with the first speaker, so I asked him why he made his daughter a schoolteacher. If schools were bad for the country, teaching surely helped to spread the rot.

He grinned and said it was nothing to do with him. He was in the bush most of the year and it was his wife who said what the children were to do. "She has education herself, and she says the children is going to have it, too."

Joe had mentioned wood carving, so I asked if he would carve me something to take home. He said he'd make me a wooden tomahawk if he could find a good enough piece of birch. The lake was still too rough for fishing, so I suggested we go off together into the woods to find some suitable birch.

"There isn't any this side of the island, because I looked this morning," he said. "We'll have to go clear across to the other side."

This suited me. A walk in the woods, with a running commentary by Joe, would be worth making.

CHAPTER VIII

NO convenient deer trails led into the bush from the camp, nor tracks of any other kind, so we had to enter by brute force, floundering through the tangled ground-vines and rotting logs underfoot and brushing aside with our hands the bushes that barred our way. I noted that Joe, in the lead, made as much noise as I. I had always imagined that Indians, like wolves, slunk silently through the bush without disturbing leaf or twig. They don't, and nor, according to Joe, do wolves, which are, he says, the noisiest creatures in the bush.

When they get together in a gang you can hear them crashing through the brush a couple of miles away.

Joe's first halt was by the side of a young balsam tree. He pointed to the pimples on the stem and said the juice inside was good for a cold. With his knife he cut round one and removed it, complete with surrounding bark. Then he punctured the soft rounded side and sucked out the white gummy liquid.

"Just like whisky," he commented and cut out another pimple for me.

I didn't suppose for a moment that it was anything like whisky, except in colour, but in the interests of science I sampled it. It tasted just like a pine tree smells, which is pleasing to the nostrils but most unpleasant on the palate. Joe saw me screw up my face with distaste, and, largely I suspect from bravado, cut off another pimple and took a second swig himself.

This balsam tree, like many of the other species on the island, had been attacked by some kind of bug. There was no sign of any insect feeding on it, but the tree was sickly and the leaves, as Joe put it, were just like porcupine quills. He said the Japanese beetle was responsible. The grubs eat the roots, he said, and the trees get sick. He reckoned these beetles had been dropped from aeroplanes by the Japs and that was why he volunteered to go to China. He had been bombed and gassed in the first war and they were things a man expected, but dropping beetles on harmless trees from aeroplanes was a dastardly thing to do.

I am reliably informed that it is not the Japanese, or any other beetle, that does the damage but the bud worm, now being successfully combated with D.D.T.

Our next stop was at a sugar maple. In my Euro-

106

pean ignorance I thought these trees provided the syrup ready made. All you had to do was tap the trunk and hang buckets out to catch the syrup. From Joe I learned the sap must be boiled until it reaches the right colour and consistency. Knowing the correct moment to stop boiling is the secret of the whole process. The first spring thaw, when the frost is getting out of the trees, is the best time to draw the sap.

On a log, beside the maple tree, curious brown fungi sprouted out, like hands without fingers. "They call that pungus," Joe said. "There's some people says 'fungus' but mostly around here it's called 'pungus.' That kind there is called shelf pungus, because you can dry it and polish it up and then nail it to a wall for a shelf."

He cut one of the "shelves" from the log with his hatchet and handed it to me. The upper side had a shiny brown skin but underneath it was covered with a white coating, like moist powdered chalk, that came off when touched.

"The old Indians used to write messages on pungus," said Joe, taking it back and scratching on the coated side with a stick, till he had sketched a sheathed hunting-knife.

"They used to make their message on the pungus and then leave it by the side of the trail. Then another Indian coming along would pick it up and look to see what was drawn there," he said.

I asked Joe if Indians ever got lost in the bush. "No," he said. "Nor need anybody else."

"Well, supposing you didn't have a compass or a map and the clouds were so thick you couldn't see the sun, what would you do?"

Joe led me over to the base of a large tree and kicked

away the top soil till he had exposed the roots. "See here?" he said. "Even if I was blind I'd know this was the north side of the tree because this is where the biggest roots grow. The biggest limbs grow out to the north too. Then there's another way you can tell, and that is by looking at the top of the big pines. You'll see they always 'kneel' to the east."

I had noticed that the tops of most big pines were bent, but I hadn't seen that they all tilted in the same direction. I said I supposed it was caused by the westerly winds.

"No," said Joe, "it's not the wind. If it was, they'd point south because the strongest winds come from the north. I don't rightly know what causes it, but I reckon it's something to do with electricity. It's well known that pines have a lot of electricity in them and that must have something to do with it."

I kept a careful watch on the tops of pines after this and I must say that on the whole Joe seemed right. They didn't all point due east but there was a definite tendency for them to do so. Sometimes when we passed one that was more than 45 degrees out I would show it to Joe and say, "Now, what?"

"Well, sir," he would say, "that tree doesn't count. It's on an island and it's well known that trees on islands are bad pointers." Or else he would say that the tree was second growth timber, a mere stripling that had sprouted up after the original trees had been felled.

"You can't expect second growth timber to kneel right," he said. "It takes hundreds of years."

"Supposing you are in country where there aren't any big trees, then what would you do?" I asked.

"I'd look for the moss on the small trees," he said.

"It grows only on the north side." Joe explained that this was to protect the tree from the north wind. It would be nice to think that moss was as thoughtful as that for its host but I believe the explanation is that strong sun kills moss and the north side of a tree is the least sunny.

"All right, Joe," I said. "We now know where we are. We're not lost. But that won't do us any good if we're a long way from home and there's a storm coming up and we haven't anywhere to go, or anything to eat and we've run out of matches."

"The first thing would be to cut some birch bark and build a lean-to shelter," said Joe.

"Ah, half a moment," I said. "We haven't got a hatchet or a knife. Only our bare hands."

"That's easy," he answered, going up to an old hardwood tree that had died on its feet, and pulling away great lengths of dried bark. "If we get enough of this it will do us until the storm goes over."

"Right," I said, satisfied from this speedy demonstration that a reasonable shelter could be built in an emergency. "Now we are hungry and we haven't a rifle or a bow and arrow. Where do we go for something to eat?"

"We might catch some minnows," Joe said. "We might build a trap in the shallows with stones and drive them in. Or we might find a partridge. He's so dumb, that fellow, you can knock him on the head with a stick. Or a porcupine. He's more dumb. Many a man in the bush has saved his life by coming on a porcupine. Then there's bull frogs. There's plenty of people eat them for pleasure."

"We don't want to eat these things raw, so how about a fire?"

"All you want for that," said Joe, "is a stone and a bit of steel to make a spark. Even if a man has nothing in his pockets he always has a bit of steel about him somewhere. Maybe it is only a buckle on his belt, or a nail in his shoe, but he'll have a bit somewhere and if you have a stone and steel you can always make a fire."

So you now know what to do if you ever find yourself lost and alone in the bush without any of the usual necessities of life. I bet you never thought of making a fire with a nail from your shoe.

We were now approaching a more open part of the wood where the undergrowth was lighter and the trees bigger. Joe went up to a tree and asked if I knew what it was.

"Silver birch," I said, remembering one I had seen labelled near the hotel.

"That's right," said Joe. "Silver birch, and that's what you get venereal from. If I had a 12-foot block of that tree and I could get it down to Toronto, they'd pay me 300 dollars for it."

"What on earth for?" I said.

Joe looked at me with astonishment. "I reckon *you* ought to know," he answered. "How would you have gone flying in this war without it? Where would you have been if those airplane people down in Toronto hadn't no venereal?"

I suppose I should have told Joe the word was "veneer" but somehow I felt it a shame to spoil the joke for the next fellow.

Near the foot of the silver birch was a moss that sent up little six-inch sprigs. Joe called it prince pine and said the boys were collecting it in the late summer to send into town. It fetched five cents a pound and was waxed and sold for Christmas decorations.

We passed many small birch trees before Joe decided on one that was good enough for cutting. It looked just the same as any of the others to me, but there must have been something about it the others hadn't got, for Joe spotted it a long way off and said, when we were still 40 yards away, that it was just what he wanted. He felled it with a few quick strokes and chopped off a couple of 18-inch lengths. He said he would carve the tomahawk from one length and take the other home. I couldn't get any very satisfactory explanation from him as to why this particular lump of wood was worth dragging all the way back to the hotel. As I remembered it the hotel was almost entirely surrounded by birch trees. Apparently it was the same with birch bark. An Indian who wanted to make a canoe was quite happy to wander through the bush for days to find just the right tree. June is the month for cutting birch bark. In July, said Joe, it becomes "brickly." You can make a birch bark canoe in a few days. He used to make one every year. He sold one once for 40 dollars, but it was a special job with a lot of Indian-style carving and decorations. Ordinarily 25 dollars was a good price.

In the days before this country was a park most of the big timber was taken out by the sweating, swearing subjects of the lumber kings. That was 50 years ago, but the stumps of the great pines had not fully rotted yet. After half a century of exposure to the frosts and the snow, to the hosts of insects and microbes which nature turns on the task of reducing wood to the mould from which it sprang, these stumps still retain their majesty beside the saplings and the second growth timber. What an elegy could be written round one of these mounds over which the ants crawl and the moss grows. The puny men who came with their axes and saws and the swagger of conquerors are buried and gone. They floundered in the snow and sweated in the sun to hack the trees down and now they have vanished into history, disintegrated in everything but name. They laughed, those men, as the forest monarchs fell and then, in death, sought to arrest their mortal decay by refuge in coffins made from the self-same trees they once despoiled. The names of the lumber men are dotted all over the map of Algonquin Park, the railways and roads they built remain, but they themselves are gone. Their useless bones are rotting underground but the timber they cut in their short hour of triumph still fills a million wants. The floor on which I walk in London, the lintel round the fireplace, the sashes of my window were made from these long-dead trees of Canada. Perhaps they came from Otterslide or Big Trout Lake. The train that takes me to work, the platform on which I stand and wait for it, the pub round the corner where I buy my beer—there is pine from Canada in all of them.

No timber is taken from the Park now. The trees are protected like the creatures, but I shall never see the difference, nor will my son or my son's son, for many men will grow and die before one of the new generation of great pines reaches its full stature.

From Christmas till early spring Joe earned his living in the timber industry. First, he said, you start as a trail-cutter and get three and a half dollars a day, then you graduate to teamster and then a roller. After that you may rise to be a "buck beaver," a "walking boss," and finally a "bishop." In the lumber hierarchy the bishop comes next to the man who owns the outfit and is paid 15 dollars a day. If you work inside the mill you may be known by any of the following names: setter, sawer, filer, edgerman, tail sawer, dogger, resawman, tie-peeler, gangsawman, bolterman, jobber, slash tableman, edgerboxman or sawdust cleanerupper. The aristocrats are the sawer (12 dollars a day) and the filer (14 dollars a day).

I asked Joe where he fitted in. He said he was an agent and got six dollars a day. "I look after the dumps," he said. Just what the dumps were or what looking after them involved I never quite understood. Whenever I tried to learn more he answered something like this: "Well, the dumps. You know what dumps are. And I look after them."

When we returned to camp from our expedition into the hinterland of our island, it was quite late in the afternoon. The wind had dropped a little, as Joe had said it might, and he reckoned we could have another go at the fish. We tried different water this time and, instead of the open lake, Joe paddled slowly round the island. My attention rather wandered from the fish, for every time we rounded a rocky headland, and there were dozens, I hoped to find a moose standing in the water. The suspense as we paddled silently round each bend was great—and each time the little bay we came upon was deserted. Yet there was always another corner ahead which might be *the one*, which might be hiding that picture I wanted so much for my memory collection. So I wasn't really paying much attention to my copper line when the big fish struck. It took the bait with a bang and in the flurry of switching my mind from an imaginary moose to a very real trout I fumbled the handle of the reel, losing precious seconds before starting to wind in.

"He'll somerset on you, he'll somerset," yelled Joe, paddling like fury.

For several agonising moments I thought I had lost him. I wound in without feeling anything on the line. Then I got his weight again and wound faster to keep it there. What I completely forgot to do was to strike so as to tighten the hook. I should have done it in the first second after he hit, but what with my day dreaming about moose and my bungling on the reel I forgot all about it. There was no doubt that this was a big one. Even with such a cumbersome outfit it was easy to tell this fish had quality. As we brought him near the canoe he bored down deep and went underneath us. Joe performed miracles with the paddle, and spun the canoe round so that we had him at the side again. He made two dashes from the canoe before Joe caught the line and yanked him from the water. And then he came off the hook. He came off in mid-air, two feet above the water, and left Joe with the bait dangling in his hand. But the jerk he had given as he pulled the fish out still gave it motion and it hurled towards the canoe, smacked down on the edge and then slid down *on the wrong side*. I caught just a glimpse of its powerful tail, curved for the sweep that sent it torpedoing down to the safety of the deep, and then it was gone.

Joe and I just looked at each other and didn't speak. He took the bait in his hand and felt the points of the hooks with his finger. He had sharpened them himself that morning, so he knew there was nothing wrong, but doing something saved having to speak.

At length he broke the silence with the two words: "Twelve pounds."

Estimating the weight of a fish that got away is one of the most profitless occupations on earth, but the day we cease to do it will be the day when we are all of us called upon to answer sterner charges than telling fishermen's tales.

Joe said 12 and I reckon about 10. When we got back to civilisation and its audiences, the weight increased, pound by pound, from 12 to 16. But still, it was a darn good fish and we almost sneered at the mere five-pounder that came in half an hour later.

Joe reckoned we were lucky to catch even this, as the wind had shifted to the south. In England a south wind is good for fishing, or at any rate I have never found it to be bad, but Joe was quite definite on this point and recited the following:

"When the East Wind blows the fish won't bite;
South Wind they bite least;
West Wind blows the bait right into their mouth;
North Wind they bite best."

There may be some reason about this, but there is certainly no rhyme. Joe thought it was terrific, and spoke each line as if it was even slicker than the one before. As a mnemonic I think it about the worst I ever heard. During the remainder of the trip I had him repeat it to me half a dozen times and still couldn't remember it. I am able to pass it on only because I finally took out pencil and paper and wrote it down to his dictation.

Although we saw no moose on this afternoon expedition round the lake shore we became closely acquainted with several loons. They make a great noise when a canoe approaches, complaining at the intrusion, and from all over the lake their fellows send their sympathy. It is apt to get on your nerves, this row, and you splash your paddle on the water to make them dive. Before they go under they send out a final cry of anguish to let the others know the worst. Joe said he saw a loon asleep on the water once with its head tucked back on its shoulder. He had a .303 rifle with him, so he fired at the water beside it. "Holy Boy, did he move quick!" said Joe. "But quick as he was he still had time to call out before he went down."

If you didn't wave your arms or bang your paddle on the water the loons would let you approach to within 30 yards before diving. Once when we drew near to one I called out, "Shut up!" and it promptly dived. Joe was delighted and said it understood me. Thereafter we used to compete with each other in judging the psychological moment to call "Shut up!" Joe was very good at it. Perhaps, with his Indian eyesight, he could see the bird getting ready for its dive.

After staying under water for half a minute or so the loon would come up behind the canoe and send out a reassuring cry, with relief in every note. Joe translated this call as, "Don't bother now. It's all right. I've chased them away."

That evening as we cooked our trout the wind slacked off and the water calmed, but 30,000 feet up wispy cirrus cloud was moving in from the west. Joe said he was certain now the weather would break and I asked him how he knew, thinking he would point to the "mares' tails" in the sky, outriders of the approaching cold front.

"I know," he said, "partly because the loons is still acting queer, and partly because this fish we're eating now had nothing inside it, and I also know because I saw the snowbird this afternoon."

"Snowbird!" I said. "Don't tell me it's going to snow in August."

"Well, sir, I only seen the snowbird as early as this once before, and when I got back to the hotel there was six inches of snow and all the guests had gone. It's a bad thing to see the snowbird."

"What does this snowbird look like?"

"It's white on top and it's grey underneath. Size? Well, about as big as a chicken."

Canadians I have asked think Joe may have meant a ptarmigan or grouse.

All evening the sky continued to cloud over until the only clear patch was a small square in the east. Joe pointed to it and shook his head. "See that handkerchief," he said. "If it was in the north there'd be some chance. But a handkerchief in the east is bad."

While Joe and I were discussing the weather in terms of "mares' tails," handkerchiefs, loons and snowbirds, the meteorologists of Canada and the States were working on their evening weather-map. The feeble Saskatchewan front of the day before had grown in 24 hours into a mighty fellow 1,800 miles wide, that stretched from the middle of Hudson Bay to the mountains of Colorado. And the local weather forecast, had we known it, was: Moderate to fresh south-west winds, partly cloudy and warm.

But it wasn't warm, and we piled the fire high that night and rolled a log in front on which we sat and swopped yarns.

"You know," said Joe, "every man has his weakness, and mostly it's a woman. There was that trapper who stole them gold nuggets. The Mounties couldn't catch him. He travelled in snowstorms to hide his tracks, he doubled back on his own trail and shot the men coming after him. He sent notes to say where he'd be and then he ambushed the police on their way to get him. Thirteen men he killed and the Mounties began to wish they'd never heard of him. But they got him in the end. And it was a woman who did it. Went out into the bush pretending she was a camper, and led him into a trap.

"There's some way to get every man. It was the same with that gangster, Baby Face Nelson. They got him and it was a woman did that. He died hard, but they got him. I saw the picture. He was on his knees pulling his gun when he went down. The girl who gave him away said to the police, 'He's going to the movies and you'll know us when we come out because I'll be wearing red.'

"Well, sir, I saw that girl on the movies and do you know what I think? I think she's the same woman that king lost his throne over. I saw *her* on the movies, too, and by Jeepers, she looked the same woman to me. She'd been married before she met that king, you know, and had a different name."

I repeat this story because I think it demonstrates the often unsuspected impact that films can have on a mind unattuned to them. Most regular film-goers wouldn't make such a mistake, but the unread Indian coming in from the bush once a year, even one as intelligent as Joe, lacks their mental immunity when exposed to the kaleidoscopic suggestions of the screen.

If Joe had been a newspaper reader he would have known that it was not Baby Face Nelson but John Dillinger who was betrayed to the police and shot to death outside the Biograph Cinema, Chicago, in July, 1934.

He would also have known that the "Woman in Red" was Anna Sage, or Sagen, deported two years later as an undesirable alien.

CHAPTER IX

THAT night was much colder than the previous two, and blankets alone were not enough. We slept in our clothes and wore our spares as well, which meant we had nothing left with which to make pillows except the pack bags and our boots. Joe slept well, and I slept some of the time. At intervals before dawn I could hear the wind in the hemlock trees around the tent and the lake water splashing on the point. Sometimes I thought I heard the patter of rain on the canvas but found in the morning it had been the needles falling from the hemlocks. Once a mouse ran up the tent outside, scratching for a grip with its toes. Perhaps it was chased by some prowler of the night, and I listened for stealthy steps but heard nothing until the mouse slid down again in a series of swishes and jolts, like someone learning to ski.

In the morning Joe broke the silence of that pleasant interval between night and day when, though you know it is time to get up, you feel nothing much will go wrong if you don't.

"There's bad news," he said, fumbling in the pack on which his head had been lying. "There's been an explosion. Yes, sir, both the flour and the sugar bags has exploded."

The sky had a wet and cloudy look about it, but no actual rain, and the wind had dropped a little. Joe reckoned it was just a lull and we should take advantage of it to catch another fish.

"If it comes on to blow bad we may be stuck on the Chrysly old island till it's time to go home," he said. "You have to play the game with weather, you know. It is not a thing to be taken lightly."

So, without waiting to wash, without even stripping the outer layer of clothing in which we had slept, we launched the canoe and let out the line. Inside half an hour we had a couple of three-pounders in the boat and were paddling hard for camp, with anxious eyes on the threatening clouds. With these two fish, and the half one left over from the day before, we were all right for food for a couple of days.

Joe reckoned we had done a wise thing, going out when we did. "There's people gets drowned every year going out in bad weather," he said. "There was those two in Dickson Lake, and the three in Lavieille and they never did find the body of that woman in Opeongo. They found her canoe but that woman was sunk."

Mugs of hot tea, with our morning bacon and eggs, put new life into us and I asked Joe, "What next?"

"I've a notion to take a walk," he said, "and I've another notion not to."

"Where would you walk, if you fixed on that notion?" I asked.

He pointed across the lake to a high sandy bluff two miles to the east. "I guess if we was to paddle round close to the island we could cut across to the main shore without getting the wind. There's two miles of sand along the lake there and all the animals that goes to the water has to cross it and leave their tracks. If we was to take a walk along it we might find out what animals is living in the Jeezly park this year. We might see if there's any fishers hiding out around here."

All I knew about fishers was that they could kill porcupines, something few animals other than man can do, and I asked for more information. Drops of rain had begun to fall, so, postponing the notion to take a walk, we retired to the tent for a lesson on fishers. Joe took with him the birchwood block he had cut the day before and he shaped it out with his hatchet as he talked.

I had come to the right man for information about fishers, for Joe had made a special study of them. There was a time, he said, when a fisher skin was worth 130 dollars and even now a good one fetched 110. The creature has long brown silly hair, Joe said, and ladies felt pretty good if they had a tie made of fisher skin. "It makes them feel they're all dressed up and walking on their toes.

"When I first started trapping I trailed a fisher for seven days and studied how he lived," he went on. "I learned his nature. I could have caught him any time, but I wanted to see what he did. He travelled in the daytime and lay up at night and did little eating, just a few mice and small things. Then he found a deer kill the wolves had left and had his first real meal in a week. In the summer he'll eat snakes and frogs and he'll dig for toads but in the winter he follows the wolves. That's what I found. I've never had to hunt a fisher since that first one. I learned enough then to trap him without going after him."

"Does he eat much fish?" I asked.

"Jeepers, no," said Joe. "He's like a cat, that fellow. Just hates getting his feet wet."

"In that case why is he called a fisher?"

"Well, sir, I've met many people round the bush called Martin, but it doesn't mean they look like an old stone marten. And I've met people who've called themselves Wolff, but they didn't look anything like a timber wolf, and there's other people called Woodcock who don't have any parts of them made of wood, so a fisher don't have to fish just because of his name."

I asked Joe the price he got for his furs and he gave me the following list. In the last column, for comparison, are the top prices paid by the Hudson's Bay Company in 1945. The figures are Canadian dollars.

	Joe's Price	*Hudson's Bay*
Mink	25	30
Beaver	50	55
Otter	40	35
Fisher	110	110
Timber Weasel	3	2
Red Fox	20	13
Grey Fox	12	12
Silver Fox	60	30
White Fox	30	30
Cross Fox	90	25
Racoon	5	5
Wolverine	35	20
Wild Cat	25	15
Lynx	50	60
Muskrat	4	3

Running your eye down the list you will see that, except for some of the foxes, where the prices can vary greatly with the quality of the skin, Joe's list was fairly accurate. He told me he subscribed to a monthly letter from Montreal giving all the market information. His daughter read it out to him. It cost 50 dollars a year but paid because it enabled him to buy furs from other Indians at less than market price.

When he gave me his price list Joe mentioned four kinds of marten, swamp (25 dollars), red pine (25 dollars), orange (35 dollars), and Stone (80 dollars). The Hudson's Bay Company said these varieties were unknown to them and must be local names.

For a wolf you get a 25 dollars bounty and for a bear 10 dollars. Joe said it took so long to get your bounty money out of the Government that he didn't bother with wolves, unless he happened to come across one. He didn't know the market price of a bearskin because any he obtained he sold privately to people in the States. He had orders for five skins in the coming winter, all from people he had been guide to in the summer.

Joe trapped in partnership with his brother Mat and between the opening of the season and Christmas, he said, he made fourteen to fifteen hundred dollars. Later on in the trip I asked him the same question again and he said a thousand dollars. Perhaps he thought I was a tax collector.

His brother continued trapping in January but Joe went to work for the timber companies after Christmas. "Trapping gets uncomfortable in the New Year. There's too much snow and you're floundering in it up to your waist as often as not." He said he was going to give it up altogether in a few seasons because his rheumatism was getting too bad. As it was he did not like to be out in the bush alone in the winter. He liked to have Mat with him wherever he went.

The best bait for a fisher or any carnivorous animal is beaver meat. Traps must be inspected at least once every eight days, otherwise the mice spoil the fur. Joe said that one time he had 300 dollars' worth of mink and fisher skins ruined in this way. Instead of inspecting the traps when he should have done, he went off 10 days guiding deer hunters. He earned 50 dollars as a guide and lost 300 as a trapper. He told me this story three times, so it evidently rankled. After that experience he organised trips for the hunters, fixed up huts and provisions for them, and then engaged lesser men to do the guiding.

We talked about furs for perhaps an hour and in that time, working with the hatchet alone, he had turned the block of birchwood into an almost perfect replica of the weapon he held in his hands. It is now used in the daily battles that go on in the street outside my window. I have told the boys who wield it that the wooden tomahawk was made by a real Indian and they show a polite interest, but I somehow feel they would rather it was a model flying bomb or a rocket. Cowboys and Indians is a dying game, in our street. It is all atomic bomb stuff these days.

The rain didn't come to anything, but the continuing threat kept us around the camp until after lunch. "It makes the day wrong," said Joe, "if you can't get out for a while."

When we did set off we called first at a small islet, satellite of our own, because Joe said there was a camp site on it and we might find something worth picking up. It was the first of three at which we called during the afternoon. The other two were those lately vacated by our dear little friends, Stinker and Co. All three camps were extremely untidy. On the back of my travel permit there were printed these words: "The good camper burns his garbage, buries his tin cans, and co-operates to maintain the travel routes and camp sites in a sanitary condition."

Apart from the cans, soap, salt, dirty rags and toilet rolls which we had found at Burnt Island Lake we also discovered the following: 4 spoons; a pair of shoes, size 6 and almost new; a toothbrush marked "Jack Rose," another marked "Derzon" and two others unmarked; a pair of dirty, but unholed, socks with the name tab of "Marc E. Limner," a similar pair marked "John B. Walsh" and *two* pairs bearing the name "David Hobart."

David, my boy, I wonder if your nickname begins with S. In clothes-rationed Europe it certainly would.

When we reached the sandy beach for which we were bound we pulled up the canoe and set off to look for tracks. After a few seconds Joe identified the trail of a wolverine. I asked him how he knew it was a wolverine. He just did, that was all, and the best I could get out of him was that a wolverine "runs along like a mink, but it's bigger."

Wolverines once figured largely in my reading. They were always finding and eating the hero's cached meat. They also ate beavers if they could get them. I always thought, in those days, that they were female wolves. Diligent research in natural history books, however, reveals that the wolverine belongs to the *Mustelidae* family, which includes badgers, weasels and minks. So Joe's comparison of its tracks and gait with those of the mink may have some scientific basis.

The wolverine had loped along the shore for 10 or 20 yards, then gone back into the bush. The next lot of tracks we found were made, said Joe, by a wild cat. He said it was an easy footprint to recognise because the claws sank so deep in the sand. "He's well known to be an ugly animal, that cat," said Joe. "If he sees you coming he will climb into a tree and jump on you when you pass. He's the only animal in the bush I'm afraid of, except the old moose at mating time."

The wild cat, like the wolverine, had stayed but a short while on the beach and then gone back to the bush. Soon Joe was pointing to another track and saying "eok."

"What's an eok?" I asked.

"Haven't you never heard of an eok?"

"Not that I can remember."

"Well, sir, an eok is smaller than a moose and bigger than a deer."

"Oh," I said, "You mean an elk."

"That's what I said, an eok."

He knew the track was made by an eok because of the size. I asked how he could be sure it wasn't a part-grown moose. There must be a period in the life of every moose when it is just the same size as an eok. I was seeking knowledge, but Joe thought I was riding him.

"Maybe I don't know what an eok track looks like? Maybe it's not an eok at all, but a jaguar?" he said testily. From then on it became a standing joke that when I asked too many questions, like a child out for a walk with its father, Joe would answer, "Jaguar." There are no jaguars in those parts, of course, and where Joe heard of them I don't know, but he told me a long and involved story of how he once saw a clipped French poodle and persuaded the man who was with him that it was a jaguar.

Suddenly, as we were walking, Joe grabbed my arm and pulled me back, with a cry of "Holy Boy! Look at that."

"That" was a series of half a dozen shallow, and roughly parallel, lines in the sand, leading from the bush and disappearing into the water.

"Rattlesnake tracks!" said Joe.

Someone in the train coming up had told me there were no poisonous snakes in the Park, so I waited for Joe to continue.

"Yes, sir," he said. "That's an old rattlesnake all right. He lives in the bush here and goes into the water for a swim every day. Just now he's in the lake. We ought to get away from here, he may come back."

A few yards out was a rock with a tree branch floating beside it. "There's the rattler," I said with mock alarm, "and there's the jaguar swimming beside it." Joe thought this very funny. I can understand that he would, for it was only an elaboration of his own joke. What I can't fathom, and never will, is why the following made him laugh till the tears came: At one of the empty camp sites we had found a saucepan lid, something we didn't possess, and we took it back to our own camp. That night Joe said, "This is just the thing we want when we make soup for supper." "That's odd," I said vaguely. "We must have known when we found it that we were going to cook soup to-night."

Now, I don't think this is very funny myself, and it is certainly not the type of joke I would make if I set out deliberately to amuse an illiterate, but Joe sat down on a log and nearly exploded with laughter. He rolled from side to side in an agony of mirth, till he had me laughing with a bellyache too. We sat one each side of the fire and it got so bad that we couldn't look at each other without going off into fits. At least twice a day for the remainder of the trip Joe remembered the saucepan lid and laughed about it all over again.

But to return to the rattlesnake tracks. They were made by the twigs of a branch that had been dragged down to the lake by a beaver. A few yards back in the bush was a small land-locked lagoon, full of dead timber, and round the edge were six or seven castoring places. Joe took a stick from one and smelled for its hidden message.

"Jeepers, that beaver's got rude thoughts," he said. "The things he'd do to a lady beaver if he got hold of her is just too bad."

Cat-like, Joe skipped from log to log on the timber floating in the lagoon and I followed until he pointed in triumph to a nasty mess of sticks and leaves in the hollow formed by two converging logs. "That's his home," he said. "He's a hermit beaver without a mate and don't think it worth while to build a proper house."

A more revolting place to call home I can't imagine. If the messages at the castoring-places were exotic he had really let himself go on the drawing-room walls.

On this tracking expedition of ours we saw signs of neither skunks nor porcupines, but Joe mentioned both. Skunks, he said, couldn't make a smell if you picked them up by the tail. He had done this once and run to the lake shore and thrown the unfortunate creature into the water. "My wife saw it," said Joe, "and yelled, 'Put it down, you must be mad.'" Of the porcupine, he said that if it was caught out in a snowstorm and couldn't find a hollow tree or log it would hang upside-down from a branch. "I've seen him like this with the icicles on his quills," he said.

There was no real rain all the afternoon and as we paddled back to camp, across the choppy open water, we both thought there was wet weather to come; Joe, from the previously noted behaviour of the birds and the beasts, and I from the smattering of meteorological lore picked up in the R.A.F. As a matter of fact we were both wrong, as the experts in the outside world with their weather maps could have told us. The great front had passed over us in the early afternoon and now stretched in a curved line from Labrador, through the Middle West and down to New Mexico. Behind it the air was cold but dry.

That night, as we sat round the camp-fire, roasted on one side and frozen on the other, the clouds thinned and at intervals the moon, two days from full, broke through and laid its silver touch upon the lake.

Joe's stories became shorter and then stopped altogether. The fire sank to a few embers we could quench with a cupful of water. Joe had turned for the tent and I for a last look at the beauty of the lake in the moonlight, when something came swimming round the point, not 20 yards from the rocks. Without a sound, almost without a ripple, it moved from the half-shadows of the island to the open moonlit water, something two, perhaps three feet long, that was a joy to watch even without knowing what it was.

"Otter," whispered Joe, who had turned and crept silently back to where I stood. He stooped to pick up a stone. I would have stopped him if I had thought for a moment, but I was too fascinated by the otter to move or speak. I saw a surfaced U-boat once, as we unexpectedly broke cloud 4,000 feet above the sea, and I remember well that it looked so natural and graceful that it seemed almost a shame to frighten it.

The otter, from 20 feet, looked awfully like that U-boat from 4,000, with the difference that there was no need to remind myself that I was there for predatory purposes and not to admire the scenery. Then Joe's stone crashed, like an exploding depth charge, an inch from the otter's stern. There was a swirl and the creature had vanished.

From round the bend came a faint animal cry, so narrowly separated from the inaudible that I wouldn't have noticed it had Joe not said, "Hear his mate calling him?"

Joe, chuckling at the accuracy of his aim, went back to the tent and I slipped down to the beach. The otter had surfaced again and I watched it, undisturbed, till it left the moonlit patch of water and faded into the gloom.

Our plans for the next day depended so much upon the weather that we went to our spruce-bough beds without deciding what we would do. If the weather was bad we would have to stay where we were, and perhaps return the way we had come, abandoning the idea of a different route home. I was loath to do this because the second half of the journey promised the best chance of seeing moose. For several miles we would be travelling through swampy country that Joe called "the mash" and where, he said, we'd see all the game we wanted. So I was glad when the morning came and the weather was at least no worse.

Joe reckoned we would try to cross the main lake and keep to the route we had originally planned. We packed up our kit and took down the tent. Our two beds of spruce looked forlorn and exposed, lying there in the open. So did the three tables, the two that Joe built and the one we inherited from the last campers. I might have been sorry to leave if it wasn't that ahead lay the promise of new lakes, new camps, other islands and four days more with Joe.

Alone I might have sweated with fear as we crossed three miles of open water with the wind from the north whipping up the water into a cross-sea that soaked us with its spray. But if Joe was happy, so was I, and when he suggested I should troll for a fish for lunch I knew that all was well. If he was prepared to paddle a loaded canoe, with 150 feet of line dragging behind, I knew there couldn't be much wrong. We caught a fish of five or six pounds 20 minutes after letting the line out. It was much darker in colour than the others and somehow didn't taste so good when we ate it for lunch. That may have been due to imagination or to the fact that I had eaten more trout in the last four days than I normally would in four years.

Just before we left the open water for the sheltered reach of an island guarding the approach to White Lake, Joe pointed to the opposite shore. In its shelter a dozen canoes were slowly working their way in the direction from which we had come. "That's the boys going home," said Joe.

They may have been messy and noisy, they may have been too young to show the guts they will need when they grow up, but somehow I was sorry to think their vacation would be over a day or two sooner than mine. If I could have had a holiday like this at their age it would have strengthened me for the rest of my life. Perhaps it had done the same for them.

As we reached the sheltered waters of the entrance to White Lake the sun came out and, for the first time in two days, we were warm again. On the right an island screened the northern wind, and on the left the timbered mainland rose a hundred feet above our heads. The passage was no more than a hundred yards wide and was dominated by a lichened rock which had about it the look of a human face. Joe said it reminded him of "that queen who wore a cloth on her head." Looking at it again, it certainly did resemble the bust of an elderly Queen Victoria.

White Lake was the headquarters of the Park ranger in whose territory we were travelling. His name was Jack and when I asked Joe if he knew him well he said, "I ought to. He was the one who took me to jail in North Bay."

Joe was jailed, he said, over a slight misunderstanding. He just happened to have the same kind of boots as a trapper who had been poaching furs in the Park and one winter day, as he was standing in a store waiting to buy bacon and flour, a ranger came in and, pointing to Joe's boot's, said "I see your tracks are all over the Park again." Joe saw red and punched the ranger in the jaw, knocking him out. For that he got three months.

"Jack don't like to be reminded that he was the man who took me up to the jail," said Joe. "But I always tell him about it when we meet. I say, 'Do you remember that time you and I went on the train together?' Jack knows I didn't have a fair deal and he don't like me to think he had anything to do with it, which he didn't."

Jack lived in a hut by the lake in a clearing that housed a thriving timber camp 50 years ago. It is still called McLaughlin Depot and a dozen wooden shacks and tables slowly fall into decay amid the long grass and the raspberry canes. When the last of the great pines had been felled McLaughlin and his men moved on, and now only the stumps in the forest and the bleaching wooden skeletons of the cabins remain. In this forgotten world, 12 miles by canoe from the nearest habitation, Jack the Ranger lives from Monday to Saturday, year after year. He has a house at Brulé Lake, where he spends the week-ends with his family. In the summer they sometimes come back with him for a week or two to ease the loneliness of his cabin. For the rest his companions are the birds and the beasts and the ever-changing lake in front of his door.

CHAPTER X

SOMEHOW Joe's stories about the rangers led me to expect a man in resplendent uniform, like the Royal Canadian Mounted Police, all brass and bright colours. But there was nothing like that about Jack. He looked more like a Mid-West farmer or a good-natured country storekeeper. He wore an old straw hat with bits of it missing, steel-rimmed spectacles that seemed to increase the blueness of his twinkling eyes, a two-days' growth of grey beard, an old blue shirt, open at the collar, and a much-patched nondescript pair of trousers. And, to quote Joe, he "went about 160 pounds."

"Hullo, Jack," said Joe. "Me and my partner here are just looking around to see where we will put our trap lines this winter."

Jack peered at us good-naturedly through his spectacles and grinned.

"Lavally, isn't it?" he said.

"You ought to know," replied Joe. "Remember the time you took me to jail in North Bay?"

Jack let that one pass and putting down a sickle he held, came up and shook hands. "Just cutting down these darn old bushes in front of the hut so I can see you go by in the winter," he said. "If a man can't see what's going on under his own nose he's not likely to know what's happening anywhere else."

Joe's come-back was that Jack had never seen him in the Park in the winter and never would, even if he cut down every tree and bush for 40 miles.

"I've heard people say, and some of them are rangers and ought to know better, that we Indians only come into the Park in the summer as guides so that we can pick out good trap lines." Joe was quite serious but Jack the Ranger just went on smiling benevolently and nodding his head.

"Well, sir," Joe went on. "what do they do about it? They say we must round up these Indians. Catch 'em with their traps and skins in the Park. So they collect all the rangers this side of Montreal and have a round-up. And who is the first man they catch?" Joe named a trapper whose forebears were clearly Teutonic. "What sort of an Indian is he? Did you ever hear of a tribe that gave away names like that? They let him off with a fine. Then they catch another, and another, and Holy Boy if they're not all Jeezly Germans, every sonuvergun. But you still hear people say it's the Indians that does the poaching."

Having got this off his chest, Joe relaxed and asked, with a grin, if there were many fishers about this year. "I could do with about 20 nice fisher skins this season," he said.

Jack didn't know about the fishers but the beavers

134

in the Park were increasing, which elicited from Joe the following affirmation: "Jumping Mexican Jesus, you're right."

The conversation having got on to beavers, both men now got down to some real talking. When I was flying in the R.A.F. we had two normal topics, women and aeroplanes. In Fleet Street, where I have worked most of my life, we talk about women and newspapers, in my local pub it is women and politics. Here in Algonquin Park the alternative to the one so honoured by time was beavers. I can remember few lengthy conversations with Joe that did not include something about beavers.

Joe mentioned the beaver houses that we had seen left high and dry by the falling water as we came into Big Trout Lake. Jack hadn't been that way for some weeks and didn't know this, but when the water rose again, he said, the beavers would be back.

"It's this hot summer that's done it," he went on. "Never had a summer like it. The lake is down by three feet and all of it gone into the sky in evaporation."

Up MacIntosh Creek, where Joe and I would be going the next day, there was a beaver dam that had been broken. Instead of trying to repair it, said Jack, the beavers started another dam 50 yards higher up. The old dam was useful to Jack because it made a good dock on which to pull up his canoe for a portage that began there. He didn't want the beavers to abandon it and make a new one, for that would mean cutting another portage track through the woods.

"I thought I'd help the beavers mend the dam," he said. "So I took the door off an old cabin down the creek and put it in the gap in the dam. But did the old beavers show grateful? No, sir, they just went on with their new dam. I put logs on the old dam. I carried stones just like I was a beaver myself until I had pretty near mended the dam as good as any beaver could. And now, just this last week I see some new sticks and leaves round the old door, so it looks as if they are going to finish it off themselves after all."

This prompted Joe to tell a beaver story, and then Jack said he found a beaver once that had spent the whole winter in a hollow log, living like a skunk. There was no lake for miles but it got sufficient water from a near-by stream.

"Well, sir," said Joe, "you may not believe what I am going to tell you, but I killed a beaver in the woods once, and when I come to look at him he was white with wood-lice and his feet and tail was all cracked, through being out of water so long."

While the two of them competed with their beaver stories I lay back on the grass and listened, trying to hold in my memory as much of their talk as I could. I'm afraid that I can give you but a poor report of it now because, lying in the sun on the sheltered shore of that lake, with the water rippling on the pebbles and loons conversing on some faraway lake in voices muted by distance, it was almost impossible to keep awake.

Sitting in London, a London so dark and cold, grim with post-war weariness, I try to unlock the mental files containing the memories of what Joe the Indian said to Jack the Ranger. But there seems to be something wrong with my filing system, for every time I turn the lock I hear the loons calling and the water rippling. I smell the wet pebbles and feel the sun beating down on my face and all of it makes me so pleasantly drowsy I forget what it is I wish to find.

However, after much perseverance and diligent

searching of the memory I am able to recall Jack telling Joe how he caught a well-known local character and his son with 55 illicit beaver skins in their camp.

He came on their traps set among the beaver lodges and after collecting some help he lay in wait from Saturday until Tuesday. "I threw the traps in the water as if they had been sprung," he said. "When the old man finally come to look at them on Tuesday I heard him say to his son, just behind him, 'Looks like we got five beavers here.' I jumps out from behind the bank and says, 'Yes, it looks like you got something all right.' Well, sir, you should have seen those two. The lad pulls a gun and points it at me and the old man holds up an axe shouting, 'Don't come near me. Don't you dare come near.'

"I knew he was an ugly man, that, because I seen him once before when he didn't know who I was. I heard him say that time that if any ranger searched him on the water he wouldn't be alive when he came to the top. So I knew he was an ugly man. That's why I got help. If he wasn't known for being so ugly I'd have done the job alone."

Jack not only got help for his ambush, but he got a tear-gas gun from the Superintendent. It was something new in the district and there hadn't been occasion to use it before. This looked like a good opportunity, seeing that the trapper was so "ugly."

"Of course, the old man didn't know I had this gas gun when I surprised him and the boy. It's no bigger than a fountain pen and didn't look like nothing in my hand. But I couldn't use it where I stood because the wind would've blown the gas back in my face. So I kept talking to them and working my way round to the windward side all the time. I says to the boy,

'Now then, son, you wouldn't shoot a man in the bush for the sake of an old beaver skin, would you?' Then the boy sees the other two men with me and he lowers his gun, but the old man is still trembling with anger. He's waving that axe about as if he's an old-time Indian going to scalp somebody. All the while I'm working my way round and when the wind is just right I let go with the tear-gas. Well, sir, you should have just seen 'em. The old man put his hands to his face and yelled, 'Don't shoot again. Don't shoot, for mercy's sake.' I told him he was an ugly man and let him know I remembered what he said the last time we met. He said he never saw me before in his life. 'Didn't you?' I said. 'Didn't you say if a ranger ever searched you on the water you'd throw him in and drown him? If you don't know me,' I says, 'I know you. I'd know that hide of yours in a tannery.' "

There were other stories of poachers, but none so graphic as this one and I recall only odd snatches and phrases now. The conversation was temporarily adjourned for lunch by a woman's shout from the other side of a small arm of the lake.

"That's the wife," said Jack. "Been staying with me for the week and been out all morning picking raspberries."

Joe and I made a fire on the beach and cooked the fish we had caught in the morning. For sweet we had great slices of raisin pie made by Jack's wife. They prompted Joe to remark that he was willing to bet we were the only campers in the bush who had pie to eat.

After lunch the ranger's wife went for more raspberries, I lay in the sun again, and Joe and Jack went on talking. Bush fires were the topic of the afternoon session.

To a bushman fires are as important as are economic depressions to a townsman. They provide the same background of anxiety, a perpetual threat to livelihood and even life, for they are so very easy to start. Although this summer was a dry one, there had not been many fires in the Park. Most of those that had been started were the fault of campers. Joe spoke of a burnt-out island we had passed appropriately named Burnt Island Lake, and Jack said it was done by two young men who left their camp-fire alight while they went off fishing. A spark flew out and lit the bush. In a few seconds the whole camp was ablaze. They saw the fire from the lake but were too late to save anything. They lost all they had, clothes, tent, kit, everything except what was with them in the canoe.

"They probably used cedar for firewood," said Joe. "That's bad, that cedar, for burning; throws out too many sparks."

There had been another fire by the railway at Brulé Lake. It was thought to have been started by a spark from a train until Jack investigated and found it was campers again. They had built a stone wall round the fireplace, as they should, but not put a stone underneath. When they left they hadn't bothered to drench the embers with water and the fire had eaten its way through the dry roots under the stones till it reached the open bush beyond.

There were other stories about fires fought day and night for a week without rest, of hasty all-night canoe trips to reach a fire before it got out of hand and of animals running panic-stricken before the flames, so terrified that they cringed round the human fire-fighters for protection.

These men of the woods have a disconcerting habit

of letting their eyes wander while they talk, as if they don't want to miss anything going on in the outside world. Quite suddenly, in the middle of saying something about fires, Jack broke off and pointed to a small clearing on the wooded hill-side across the lake. "See that bit of white there?" he said. "That log with the bark torn off. Know what done that?"

Joe said, "Bruin."

"That's right. The old bear done that, looking for ants. Only just noticed it. Wasn't there yesterday." And then, without more ado, Jack continued the conversation where he had left off, but his eyes, I noticed, continued to rove, looking for more signs of bear or beaver or deer.

I had often noticed Joe doing the same thing, but he went one better and let hs ears rove, too. He would appear to be listening quite intelligently to what I was saying and then quite suddenly remark, "Hear that? Beaver kitten calling its mother." I would listen intently for several moments and hear absolutely nothing and then the minute I resumed talking Joe would say, "Hear it? There it goes again."

I suppose it is a gift you acquire in the woods. Perhaps it is a blessing we don't have it in more civilised parts. It would be a great strain making polite conversation and listening at the same time to what the neighbours were saying next door.

Once when Joe and I were fishing a mile or more from the lake shore, he stopped paddling and listened with his head cocked to one side. I couldn't hear a thing except the water dripping from his paddle.

"Thought I heard a fox," he said, "but I guess it is only some old can bumping against the pebbles."

I thought this was far-fetched, but on the way home

we passed an old camping site, and in the water beside it was an old can banging on the pebbles just as Joe had described. I noticed it at two hundred yards. Joe had heard it a mile off.

Another time we were trolling for fish backwards and forwards past an island. As we came near for the second time, Joe said, apropos of nothing, "That's where the bear was working."

"What bear?" I said.

"Why, the old bear that was in the bush when we come past the first time."

"Never saw it. Why didn't you point it out?"

"I didn't see it neither," he said. "But I heard it. Making a noise like a street car in the city that bear was. Don't you never hear nothing?"

The ranger suggested we should stay for the night and camp in one of the old logging-huts. Joe would have liked that too, because he was still certain the weather was going to break, but I wanted to make that promised evening trip up into the mash. If we stayed at the lumber camp, we would have 10 miles paddling, there and back, and I thought it better to find a nearer camp site.

Jack told us there was a hut abandoned by the rangers about half-way between the lumber camp and the mash. A natural spring rose out of the hills behind and ran down into the lake. This sounded good, so we packed our kit in the canoe and set off. The ranger's wife was upon the hill-side picking raspberries, and we shouted to her our thanks for the raisin pie, but she didn't hear and went on picking.

Across the lake the timbered hills rose steeply for several hundred feet. From the canoe on the water you could see nothing but foliage and an occasional rock, but from under those trees a hundred pairs of eyes, lit by fear or curiosity, must have been looking out as we paddled by. In the old days, some of those eyes might have belonged to hostile Indians, out for scalps and revenge. At any moment a bone-tipped arrow might come whistling out from the trees and war cries echo round the shores, but now the eyes that peered at us belonged to that bear of Jack's, harmlessly turning over logs for ants, to nervous deer with speckled fawns nosing at their flanks, to otters disturbed as they played on their slide and to skunks strolling aloof along the deer trails.

Even though the unseen eyes gazing down on us were far from predatory, it gave one a feeling of nakedness and exposure to be sitting there so openly in the canoe.

This is one of the aspects of "cowboys and Indians" that doesn't strike you when you play the game as a child. Whether it was your turn to wear the cowboy outfit or put on the feather head-dress you always felt you had the drop on the other fellow, and even if you were successfully ambushed by an enemy hiding behind a garbage can or a pile of timber, the results were never so dire that they stayed in the memory. But the men who played "cowboys" with the Indians 150 years ago had no such feeling of security. They had plenty of those memories that dry the mouth and make the heart beat faster. If they were successfully ambushed, it wasn't a case of beating a hasty laughing retreat, or running home to mother. They were killed, captured and tortured, and their homes burned down. When you couldn't cross a lake without wondering if an arrow or a lead slug would greet you at the other side, it must have been hard to appreciate the beauty of the scene.

I had the same feeling flying in the war. We might be up in that wonderful world three and four miles above the earth where the mountains are clouds, the sea is a purple haze, and everything is clean and soft and ethereal, but dare we revel in this beauty? Give ourselves up to its charm? You bet we daren't for at any moment a Focke-Wulf 190 might have come whizzing down out of the sun, and instead of beer in the mess that night, we might have been lining up for harp lessons. You don't have much time for the beauties of the upper air if you've ever been jumped by a Hun and seen the tracers flicking past like incandescent dotted lines. You are too busy wondering if a German fighter is behind that cloud, or under your tail. And that, I expect, is how the first trapper felt as he paddled across White Trout Lake, as Joe and I were doing so fearlessly now. Maybe one of Joe's Algonquin ancestors was the watching Indian in the bush, and it is not beyond the bounds of belief that one of his French forebears was that first venturesome trapper. Now the two factions had buried the hatchet, and the result was our Joe. If only the rest of us could resolve our enmities as satisfactorily as this . . .

Other thoughts were going through Joe's mind. As we rounded the high bluff of trees and rock, we came to a clearing similar to, but smaller than, the one round the old logging-camp. The map said it was called Mackey Farm, though it was obvious that no one had farmed there for more than a generation. If Mr. Mackey had children, they had found other pastures.

"This is the place," said Joe suddenly, as though I was expected to know what was running through his mind.

"What place?"

"Where I took them horses across the lake on a rig."

"How long ago was that, Joe?"

"Oh," he said, "40 or 50 years."

Joe was as hazy on dates as figures. If he had been 56, as he said, and he took the horses across 50 years ago, then he was only six at the time; and if it was 40 years ago, then he was 16, two ages of youthfulness that are not likely to be confused. However, if he didn't remember when it was, it had certainly left a vivid impression. The horses were needed for some work in the bush, and Joe had brought them out along the old wagon road from Brulé Lake to Mackey Farm, and then built a "rig" to take them across the lake.

"What sort of a rig did you build, Joe?"

"Like a raft," he said. "I made it from logs and put a fence round it so the horses wouldn't fall off. They were good, those horses. Didn't give no trouble at all. And in the fall I took them back on the same rig. Just needed a bit of mending work, but it was a good rig."

A small incident in the affairs of man, but it had stuck in Joe's memory for 40 years, or was it 50?

We were now in a new arm of the lake with wild hills on the left and more open country on the right. This was where the forgotten Mr. Mackey had tried, and perhaps failed, to make a living in those roaring days when McLaughlin and his lusty men made the woods ring with their oaths and their axes.

Jack has told us we would find the abandoned hut just below an island at the narrowest part of the lake. We found the island, but though I scanned the lake shore thoroughly, I could see no sign of a hut, or anywhere that a hut might be. We paddled on for another half-mile about two hundred yards off the shore, with me saying nothing about the hut not being there, for I had a feeling that Joe could see it all the time. Events proved me right, for without preamble, Joe remarked that the roof didn't look too good and someone had taken away the door.

"What roof? What door?" I asked.

"Why, in the old cabin Jack was talking about," said Joe, nodding his head vaguely towards a point on the shore half a mile ahead.

Still I couldn't distinguish a hut from the bush and derelict timber along the shore-line, and I said so.

"Well, sir," Joe said, "I've been around for a good many years, and I've been a good many places, and it doesn't seem reasonable to me that a man who can fly around in an airplane at night and see a Jerry airplane two or three miles away in the dark, it don't seem reasonable, I say, that he can't see a Jeezly old ranger's cabin half a mile in front of his nose in God's broad daylight."

Without going into the intricacies of radar, there seemed no answer to this elemental logic, so when Joe added, "Maybe you're like the old night owl, you don't see so well in daylight," I agreed that might be the answer.

Joe used to say his eyesight was spoiled by gas in the war, but it always seemed to me phenomenal. In the winter, he said, he wore contact lenses. He called them "intact glasses," and said they did not get snowed up or freeze to the nose like spectacles. They cost him 125 dollars in Toronto. At first he had a solution which formed bubbles between the glass and the eyeball, but when he complained, the doctor gave him another solution which caused no trouble.

The cabin was in a little clearing among the hemlocks 20 yards back from the lake. Instead of being made of logs, as a self-respecting cabin in the wilds should be, it was built of sawn timber, and the roof was covered with that tarred felt stuff that you put on henhouses and bicycle sheds. In front was a veranda, or the remains of one. Someone had taken the steps away, and someone else had put a soap box in their place. All the glass from the windows had gone and the roofing was ragged and torn. It wasn't at all my idea of a romantic little hide-out in the woods.

CHAPTER XI

INSIDE, the cabin was even less romantic. There were two old bedsteads—one made of wood and sacking, the other of iron—a ruined stove half of which had been removed to the beach, piles of tins left behind by campers and a great deal of mess made by mice. In one corner a porcupine had evidently been done to death, for the floor was thick with its quills, and I think, from the smell, a skunk must have ended its days there too.

Joe took one look at the place, said nothing would make him sleep there, and at once started a systematic search to see if there was anything worth having. On one wall were signs that a telephone set had been wrenched away and the copper wires that once connected the cabin with the great wide world now hung bare and useless.

Joe took them in one hand, and winding an imaginary handle with the other, pretended to call up the ranger.

"That Jack?" he said. "Well, sir I don't think much of this lousy old cabin of yours. I reckon one of your Jeezly beavers could build a better house than this."

He put down the wires, chuckling at his own humour, and came out on to the veranda. "I told that old ranger what I thought of his cabin," he said.

If the building was a disappointment, no one could complain at the setting. It was lovely. The wooded hill rose up behind with a narrow, grassy path running out of sight between the trees. The small clearing was a glory of wild flowers—golden-rod, raspberry, clover and half a dozen other kinds I didn't know. There were baby Christmas trees in different stages of infancy from six inches to several feet, wild strawberries, and jolly red clusters of bunchberries. I knew bunchberry was their name, because a patch of them outside the hotel had been labelled, but out of curiosity I asked Joe what they were called, and without hesitation he said, "Pigeon berries." Whatever their name, they are a great adornment to the bush. The plant grows a few inches high and has a small white flower, followed by a cluster of four or five scarlet balls the size of holly berries.

The hills sheltered the cabin and the lake from any wind and the south-west afternoon sun made life seem warm and lazy and comforting. Even Joe, who didn't like the heat and was plainly a little peeved that his predicted bad weather hadn't shown up, had to admit that it was a good camp site, "with a review of the lake that beat them all." He was as delighted as a school-boy with the natural spring in the woods behind the cabin. It gurgled out from the side of the hill and trickled down to the lake on a bed of mossy rocks. At one time it had been taken to the cabin on a conduit of hollow logs but this was now rotted and boken up by bears in search of grubs. Joe and I had a good drink at the spring, going down on our hands and knees in the wet moss. Joe reckoned he preferred it to liquor.

After a thorough inspection we decided to pitch the tent in front of the cabin. Joe set off with his axe to cut tent poles and I went for a bathe. The shore in front of the camp was too stony for comfortable bathing so I walked along it looking for a suitable rock or stretch of sand. Very soon I was involved in a mangled mass of dead timber washed up by some forgotten storm. Derelict trees a hundred feet long lay tangled together like giant spillikins and the only way to make progress was to find a trunk that lay pointing in the right direction and walk along it until an opportunity came to transfer to another. It was laborious, but had the advantage of silence, for my rubber-soled running shoes made no sound on the timber. I had hopes that I would surprise some wild animal and that is what happened. A small brown creature popped up at my feet and ran along the log until it came to the end, crossed a stretch of sand a couple of feet wide, leapt on some more timber and disappeared into the bush.

I've never seen a mink, except on Fifth Avenue and such places where a man is less interested in the mink than what is inside, but with no more than this passing acquaintance I felt certain the animal scuttling away in front of me was one of those much-sought-after creatures for whose skins men will face death and women something worse. For one thing it looked just like a mink should look—a miniature fur coat on legs. If Joe had been there he would have known at once, and I could have written in my note-book as follows: "Seen one mink (alive)." As it was, I might never know for certain.

I hurried back to where he was preparing the camp and in great excitement described the animal.

"And it was about six inches long and had a fluffy tail," I panted. Joe didn't seem very impressed. "Maybe," he said, "it was a flying squirrel."

That was not the answer I wanted. No one would be very interested in a flying squirrel. But a mink on the hoof was different. That really was something to talk about, specially to a lady. And now here was this Indian robbing me of my mink and substituting a flying squirrel. He must have noticed my face drop, for he said hadn't I never heard of a flying squirrel? I hadn't, as a matter of fact, but I had heard of flying foxes in Australia and the brother of a girl I know wrote a book about them. They eat fruit and they're a pest, like so many other things in Australia. There is a stuffed one in the South Kensington Natural History Museum. I told Joe this and he spat contemptuously.

Pausing after each word so as to make quite sure that I understood, he said derisively, "Foxes don't *fly*."

"They do in Australia," I answered.

"Well, sir, in the last war I met many Chrysly Australia's—that's what they call Aussies, you know—and after listening to some of the darn silly things they said about the bush I can tell you every one of them's a liar. See here, it isn't sense. You have to use your head when you study the wild animals. I know more about foxes than most men around these parts. I've studied their habits and I've trapped hundreds and hundreds of them, grey foxes, red foxes, black foxes, and white foxes, every kind of fox there is, and never seen one yet that looked as if it would ever even try to fly."

We dropped the subject of the aeronautic abilities of foxes and returned to the mink. I repeated my estimate of size as six inches, not counting the tail, and asked if that was too small or too big for a mink, or what. He said, "Well, sir, it is not too big and it is not too little. At this time of year they come in all sizes. There's large ones that are grandfathers two or three times over, and there are middlin' minks just learning the facts of life, and then there are little baby minks that has never seen the snow and only know the bush in summer. Yes, sir, they come in all sizes, just like jaguars—and foxes that fly."

After some persuasion Joe returned with me to the spot where I had seen the creature. We thought it might have left tracks and, fortunately for me, that is just what it had done. In the two-foot stretch of moist sand it had crossed were six perfect pad marks. Joe looked at them and without hesitation said, "Yes, sir, that's a mink. That's him all right. Couldn't be anything else but a mink."

Then, embarrassingly, he discovered some other tracks crossing the sand a few feet from the mink marks. He looked up at me accusingly with his brown Indian eyes and pointed a wrinkled, scornful finger at the new discovery.

"Squirrel, just a squirrel. Get down off that log and take a look at it. See? See how the toes sink in? See those claw marks? You never saw a mink that made marks like that, now did you? No, sir, that's a squirrel. Just a plain common old ordinary squirrel."

"But, Joe," I protested, "my mink didn't cross the

sand here. He crossed back there where you *said* the tracks were made by a mink. And anyway, I know the difference between a mink and a squirrel, I'm sure I do."

"Well," he said. "You know more than a lot of fine ladies do up in Montreal and New York, and it's my opinion that a man who can believe foxes fly will make himself believe anything he wants to. How long since you seen this flying mink or jaguar or whatever it was?"

"Not half an hour ago," I said. "Or less. Perhaps only 20 minutes. I came straight back to you after it ran into the bush right by that stump there."

Joe looked at the two sets of tracks again and straightened up with a shrug of the shoulders. "Maybe you did see a mink," he said. "It crossed this sand within the hour, but that old squirrel, he went by some time this morning."

I asked Joe whether we might see it again if we sat still on a log and kept quiet. "No, sir," said Joe. "Your old mink is quite a traveller. He's half a mile along the shore by now, or else he's way up in the bush huntin' birds and even if he wasn't you wouldn't see him again, not now that he knows you're here. You may think you're keeping quiet but you can't stop breathing, can you? And you can't stop your heart beating, can you now?"

I had to admit that those were drastic steps to take.

"And if you could keep quiet you couldn't stop smelling, could you?" Joe continued relentlessly.

"No," I said humbly, "I don't suppose I could."

"Of course you couldn't," said Joe. "No human can stop smelling and nor can any Jeezly animal either. You smell. I smell. That old mink up there in the bush, he smells terrible. The only difference between you and him is that he smells with his nose and you smell all over."

Joe roared with laughter at his own joke and slapped the log on which we were sitting. "Yes, sir," he said. "That old mink sure has a nose on him. Even if he wasn't to hear you, even if he wasn't to see you, he could smell you with this wind blowing off the lake even if you was to have a swim and wash yourself from the head down with soap."

"Tell me some more about minks," I said. "What do they eat?"

"Well, sir," said Joe, "he eats most things. Most things that are small and alive. Up in the bush there, he will eat just like a weasel. He'll eat maybe a mouse and then perhaps he'll see a bird sitting on a log and he'll eat that too. He's just like us. He likes a change but if he's hungry he'll take what's going, frogs, tadpoles, any darn thing he can get his teeth into. Sometimes he takes a notion to eat fish and then he's like an otter, only he can't swim as well as an otter, not as fast."

"Where does he live?"

"Oh, he lives almost any place. Sometimes he makes a nest in a hole in the ground. Sometimes he lives right in among the driftwood in just such a place as this."

Since returning to England I have had another encounter with live minks and I am able to confirm Joe's statement that they can smell terrible. There was an exhibition of them at the London Zoo. Nine wire cages in a room and a large notice saying "These animals like silence"—that plus the smell constituted the exhibition. The minks themselves stayed out of sight in their sleeping-boxes.

I went off for my swim and Joe had the camp fixed

up to his liking when I returned. He had pitched the tent in front of the cabin, using one of the veranda posts instead of a pole. When Joe put up a tent he would remove the larger stones and bushes from the site, but minor growths were allowed to remain. This time there were half a dozen little Christmas trees, about six inches high, growing in a neat row, like headposts to our spruce and balsam bedding.

The inevitable table was down on the beach, made of timber taken from the cabin, and he had put the top of an old iron stove on the fireplace. He showed me, proudly, how he could boil three pots on it at once. What with this, and the spring water, Joe reckoned it the best camp we'd had.

The only drawback was the shortage of spruce and balsam for making bedding. "The bugs has pretty near ate it all up," he said. And then to comfort me, should I find the bed too hard that night, he said it wouldn't be as bad as once in France when the only bedding he could find was two dead Germans in the mud. He slept on one, he said, and used the other for a blanket. This choice little reminiscence of war reminded him again of the "big compression" with all the "wounded and cripply men walking about with no jobs and no legs."

"If the Government does the same thing this time," said Joe, "I think I'll have to be king and put things right."

"That will be fine," I put in. "Then you'll be able to give me a job in the woods."

"Yes," he answered. "I'll give you a damn fine job. I'll give you a job in the fire-watching tower, with nothing to do but look out of the window and a nice blonde secretarial going about 120 pounds, to answer the phone."

153

Around eight in the evening we set off for our trip into the mash. The map showed that there was about four miles of it, with a width in some places of nearly a mile. Surely, somewhere, amid all that desolation, we ought to see a moose. I'd asked Jack about our chances. He went up it twice a week and sometimes more, but he was non-committal. He said that he always went up with an outboard motor these days and never saw a thing. The sound of the engine frightened the animals away, but in the days when he used to paddle his canoe he pretty nearly always saw something, a deer or an otter or more rarely a moose.

Back at the hotel when Joe and I first discussed our route he had reckoned our best chance of seeing wild life would be on the creek between Otterslide and Big Trout Lake, and the mash here was the next best bet. The Otterside part of the trip had produced only one beaver, thanks to Stinker and his little friends. But now they were miles away, and on this, the fifth day of our expedition, we were alone in the wilds at last. So I hoped we were really going to see something. Joe seemed almost as pleased to make the excursion as I and explained that even though the animals were protected he still got a hunter's thrill out of seeing them.

At eight o'clock in August hereabouts the sun hasn't set, but it is low in the sky and was so dazzling on this evening that the whole of the western skyline was like mirrored fire. It hurt to look at it, and as we paddled south into the mash, we both had to turn our faces away to the left. There might have been a bull moose standing a hundred yards off on the right for all we knew. We wouldn't have seen it. It wasn't until the sun finally went down behind the low hills that we could look around us and see what manner of country we were in.

The mash just here was really an inland delta where the sluggish MacIntosh Creek oozed into the White Trout Lake. Generations of beavers had built dams, only to abandon them when the stream moved to a-nother bed among the weeds and rotting vegetation. Millions of creatures, birds, beasts and fish, had lived and died here in the course of centuries and left their remains behind. The whole place, in fact, stank like a midden, which is what it was. Joe used a shorter word that was rather more rude, but certainly apt.

It became increasingly difficult to pick out the course of the main stream after the sun went down and we were constantly finding ourselves stranded on banks of evil mud, covered by an inch or two of water. The paddles stirred black whirlpools of muck at every drip and brought up with them gusty smells even more horrid than the pervading odour of wet rot.

Why animals should choose such a place to live when there are deep-water lakes and clean woods within a few miles is hard for a layman to understand. I suppose it is a matter of taste. Either you like it or you don't.

The green brush flourishing in the slime provides food for the beavers and the beavers make meals for the wolverines. There is good feeding for the fish and that brings the otters. Frogs like the place and that brings the cranes and the owls. Ducks find it a home from home, and they attract the foxes. Water lilies flourish and in search of their tasty roots come a host of creatures, from muskrats to moose. And to catch a glimpse of the gourmets came Joe and I, who might have been sitting comfortably round a camp-fire, smoking and telling yarns.

CHAPTER XII

THE first wild creature we saw in this wilderness of weed and water was a crane which rose from the reeds ahead and ponderously flapped away into the gloom. In the twilight it looked enormous, and to the frogs it must have seemed like a thousand-bomber raid going over. Some way off we could hear ducks talking to each other. Joe said they were black ducks, though how he knew I can't imagine. I'm not much good at languages and all ducks sound alike to me.

There were alien objects and shadows in the reeds that at first sight seemed to be deer or moose, standing knee-deep in the water, and half a dozen times I said "Hst" to Joe and pointed. But what I saw always turned out to be a rock or some grotesque tree stump. Joe began to tire of my constant false alarms and after a while didn't bother to look where I pointed but just grunted. "Another jaguar." Imagination and twilight combined to play strange tricks. If we had been in Africa instead of Canada the rocks that seemed to be deer would have looked like zebras and the old tree that was the image of a moose might have been an elephant. When my pilot and I were on dusk patrol during the war we saw all kinds of curious, and sometimes terrifying, things during that eerie period between sunset and darkness. There were fleets of enemy bombers which turned out to be specks of dust on the windscreen; we saw barrage balloons where no such things existed, flak bursts when no one was shooting at us, and once we were both of us quite certain we could see an extinct zeppelin cruising majestically below us. It turned out to be our own shadow cast by the evening moon on the clouds below. So when Joe stopped paddling and whispered "Hst" himself, it was my turn to say "Jaguar."

He pointed ahead and a hundred yards away, where the course of the stream joined the shadows, a ripple in the water was moving towards us. Joe whispered, "Beaver," and sat silently waiting for it to approach. The first beaver we had seen on the trip came within 10 feet of the canoe in broad daylight, so in the gloom I fully expected this fellow to bump into us. Instead of that, he dived with a mighty splash quite 50 yards away.

"He smelled us," said Joe.

Until that moment I had forgotten all about scent. The wind was practically unnoticeable, just a chill feeling at the back of the neck, but enough to warn that beaver 50 yards away.

The splash put up another crane from the reeds close by, and from the distant woods in the east came the hoot of an owl. This sound had the most electrifying effect on Joe. With a happy chuckle, he dug his paddle in the water and sent the canoe forward with such a surge that the ripples gurgled from bow to stern. "Hear that?" he said delightedly, the beaver forgotten. "That's the old night owl. He knows there's bad weather coming. When he calls like that you can look out."

I always thought an owl hooted because he was hungry, or lonely. The idea that he was broadcasting a weather warning was new.

"Do you mean to tell me," I said, "that the owl doesn't hoot unless there is bad weather about?"

"Mostly," said Joe, climbing down a little. "Mostly

it means a storm coming. But he is not always right, that fellow. Sometimes he's a bit off."

We paddled on in silence for a bit, and then, right beside the canoe, there was a crash like a depth charge going off. I could feel myself lift an inch from the seat with fright.

"What in hell was that?" I asked as the circle of ripples widened around us.

"Just a beaver," said Joe, laughing. "Sitting on the bank there, and didn't see us till we was right on him."

"Why didn't he smell us, like the other one?"

Joe sighed wearily and made no reply. When the course of the stream we were following had changed its direction, he had unconsciously noted that the wind was no longer at the back of his neck, but on the side of his face. Such subtleties had escaped me. They shouldn't have done, because with flying you acquire a sixth sense about the wind without the advantage of being able to feel it on the face. You unconsciously note the way the smoke is blowing, the waves on the water, the shape of the clouds and the ripples on the cornfields. Even at night, with none of these visible signs, you still have a general idea of what the wind is doing. How, I don't know, but it comes with experience.

After this surprise from the beaver, I tried to keep track of the wind myself as we wound through the mash with the stream. The next time Joe whispered, "Hst," and I saw the tell-tale arrow-head of ripples the first thing I thought of was the back of my neck. Yes, the wind was behind, and any moment the beaver would dive. That is what it did, I am glad to say. I would have been quite upset had it come to the edge of the canoe without scenting us.

This night that we went into the mash was the night before the full moon. When the glow in the west was still turning from red to grey, the moon came up in the east and cast its cold light on the desolate scene. The air grew chilly and neither of us had coats. But we paddled on without question because, with the setting of the sun, something had happened to this swamp we were going through. It had come to life. Though no living creature was in sight, the whole place seemed to pulsate. There were gurgles at the edge of the water, rustles among the reeds, and sound waves that you could sense, but not hear, seemed to fill the air.

It was a very thrilling experience, and Joe, who was nearer to nature than I, seemed in tune with every wave-length, missing nothing. He laid his paddle across the canoe and listened-in to nature, like a man with invisible earphones. In such surroundings, it is difficult to know when feeling ends and hearing begins, but at one moment I was certainly conscious of something that almost became sound, though from whence it came I couldn't tell.

"Beaver kittens," whispered Joe. "Calling their mother."

I held my breath and strained to catch the sound again, but all I heard was the beating of my own heart.

Again there may have been a sound, or there may not, but I felt the canoe tremble as Joe lifted his arm to point at the water a few yards away. A line of tiny bubbles no bigger than the silver balls on a birthday cake led in a line from the opposite bank to half-way across the narrow stream.

They passed our bows, going towards a clump of weeds on the low bank beside us, not 10 feet away. A foot from the bank they stopped and breathlessly

I waited to see the swimmer emerge. But nothing happened. The last of the bubbles burst as soundlessly as it had risen and the water was still again. Then from the reeds came a sound almost startling in its clarity, a sound like a man with a cold, sniffing to clear his nose. Right beside us, so near that I could have touched the spot with the paddle, there was another sniff, and then an ever-so-slight movement of the reeds. The rustling and the sniffing continued, but in the gloom I saw no further movement in the reeds.

For several minutes Joe and I sat there motionless in the canoe, while the two otters blew their noses beside us. I tried to feel which way the wind was blowing, but there seemed to be none. I wet a finger and held it up. It was equally cold all round. And all the time the otters snuffled in the reeds, almost in reach of our hands. Then there was silence again and presently the bubbles reappeared on the stream, going in the direction of the opposite bank.

Joe dipped his paddle and with one stroke sent the canoe skimming to the other side. We saw nothing. We heard only a movement of the reeds that grew fainter until there was no sound left at all. Joe sat listening for a full minute after I had ceased to hear anything, then said, "Well, sir, I guess they don't want to meet us."

By this time we had penetrated some two miles into the mash. The moon was high enough in the sky to put a gleam on the water without help from the western sky. It was very chilly, sitting there without jackets. Joe reckoned it was time to go home.

"If that storm comes up," he said, "we won't have

no moon to help us find the way out. I'd hate like hell to have to follow this stream without a moon."

On the way back we saw more beavers in the distance and had another one depth-charge us from the bank. We also got quite close to a couple of muskrats which dived, like beavers when they saw us, but made less fuss about it.

We didn't see a moose, we didn't see a bear or a deer. We saw no foxes, wolverines or martens. We did not actually see an otter, but it was an experience that I am never likely to forget, a communion—with Joe as the priest.

His summing-up of the trip was one that I could endorse. He said, "Holy Boy! Is there some game in that mash, or isn't there?"

We emerged into the lake again, heading north, and I didn't like to mention it at first, but I began to see things. Out there in the bush, a hundred miles from a real city and with the war over more than a week, I saw searchlights in the sky. They were a long way off, but they were there, thin white fingers of light without beginning or end. I've seen thousands in my time, and regarded them with either fear or favour, according to whether they were Jerry's or ours.

I kept the thing to myself as long as I could, but they were so unmistakable that at last I had to ask Joe if there were any big military camps or airfields to the north. Not that he knew of, he answered, and asked why.

"Oh, nothing," I said. "Just thought for a moment I saw a searchlight."

To my relief he answered, "Well, sir, I've been seeing them too, and I've been trying to figure out what they are, and do you know, sir, I think they must be the northern lights." I was glad to join him in his belief.

"There is very bad weather coming when you see those," he went on. "When you see them in the summer like this, it sure means there's one Godamighty helluva storm coming from somewhere."

With the lights flickering in the north, and the night chill raising goose pimples on my arms and legs, I was ready to believe anything.

Joe was in very high spirits as we paddled the rest of the way across the lake to where our tent stood out, like a white beacon, in the blackness of the woods.

"The colder it gets," he said, "the happier I feels and the more clothes I takes off. Yes, sir when it gets cold you won't see me going around in these thick underpants. There's some sense in bleaching yourself in the cold, but that sun is a dangerous fellow. I don't see no sense in letting him get you. He don't improve your looks any."

So that, fellow palefaces, is what the red man thinks of your hard-won sun-tan. If one is brown already, there is no merit in mahogany. It's the sallow city slicker who makes the squaws look round.

As soon as we had landed and dragged the canoe up on the beach, Joe began to collect logs and driftwood and come paddling down here in his canoe and think of November or Independence Day.

"I'm going to build the biggest fire that ever one man told another about," he said. "It's going to be so big that old Jack the Ranger will get out of his bunk and come paddling down here in his canoe and think the whole Park is gone up."

There is no fuel problem in the bush, and in a very few minutes we had collected a pile of timber on the beach about six feet high, most of it so old and dry that it lit like tinder.

Joe, 56 years old and a grandfather, danced round it doing a strip-tease act as he went, until he was left with only his pants and his boots. The flames grew higher, and his lithe brown body gleamed like polished copper as he chanted a wild and extempore song in a mixture of English, French, and what I suppose was Algonquin Indian.

I know little French and no Algonquin, but the theme of his song was easy to follow. It was a mixture of rejoicing at the coming change in the weather and a challenge to Jack the Ranger to come and put the fire out. Transcribed into Hiawathan metre, it ran something like this:

> Koko'koho, the owl has told me,
> Hooting in the trees and branches.
> Mahng, the Loon, the diving clownbird,
> By his antics and his flying,
> Mahng makes known that she is coming,
> She, the storm brought by the brothers,
> Wabun and Kabibonokka
> Wabun, East Wind, cold and icy
> Old Kabib, his northern partner
> Keego whom I ate for dinner,
> *Poisson* Keego he knew also,
> By his fasting Keego told me
> That the storm of storms approaches.
> In the sky, the Northern outlook,
> Ishkoodah, the bright light flickers.
> Ishkoodah, the northern nightlight
> Tells old Joe that Wabun's coming,
> Tells old Joe to take his shirt off
> So that Wabun's blast can bleach him.

All of which fills Joe with passion
Makes him hot with joy and daring
Thinking of the cold that's coming.
Makes him challenge all and sundry,
Makes him call to Jack the Ranger,
Jack the ancient forest fireman,
Makes him call across the water
"Come and put this Jeezly fire out,
"Come and see what Joe has started,
"Joe the mighty trapper built it,
"Joe the guide and Indian hunter,
"Joe the man who killed the Germans,
"Shooting from a factory chimney;
"Shooting down all day at Jerry.
"Come and show if you're a fireman,
"Show us how you jump like crazy,
"Jump and stamp when sparks are flying,
"Beat the flames with hemlock branches,
"Little will your skill avail you. . . ."

Those, I repeat, were not his exact words, but they convey something of his meaning and spirit.

The flames from the great fire waved their red and yellow tongues far above his head and spurted sparks that drifted up into the night. The circle of light, of which we were the centre, stretched out for 50 yards and brought within its orbit the ruined cabin and the hemlocks behind. Like the moon, a fire has a forgiving light that does not reveal the uglier side of man. In such a setting the cabin that seemed so sordid in daylight looked everything it should be, nobly built and nobly placed. There was romance in the green canoe drawn up on the shingle that belied its factory origin and even the unwashed dishes on the camp table seemed, in the flickering light, to be loaded with bear steak and moose.

Presently Joe stopped his war dance and took a long swig from the water bottle he had filled at the spring, spitting contentedly when he finished. Then he sat down on the log beside me, grinning from ear to ear, and said, "Well, sir, that's what the cold does to me. I begin to live again. Give me the snow and the ice where a man knows where he is. This summer heat may be fine for little schoolboys making themselves think they are bushmen but it is no weather for a real man."

I was going to make some reply but I saw that far-off look in his eyes and his head was tilted slightly to one side, catching some sound I couldn't hear.

"Listen!" he breathed in a whisper that was almost ecstatic. "It's the wolves!"

I listened too, and quite honestly I don't think I heard a thing, but in that setting it was so easy to imagine things that I shall never be quite sure whether I heard the wolves or not.

Joe sat there in a trance, drinking it in as if it were harp music from the clouds.

"Yes, sir, it's the wolves," he repeated. "Now I know we shall have a storm. The wolves know. You can't fool them. Maybe the old night owl is a bit off sometimes and the loon too, but not the wolves. They're always right. There is dirty weather coming. Maybe not to-morrow, nor the next day, but it is coming. There's people in the bush as will say when they hears the wolves howl, 'Those wolves has killed another deer.' But I know why they howl. It's because there's dirty weather coming and you'd better look out."

It was the perfect ending to Joe's day. The loons,

the owls, the northern lights and the ducks had all told him that the hot weather would break and now the wolves, his infallible wolves, had confirmed it for him. There was nothing more to be said on the subject and so he picked up his discarded clothes, climbed up the bank to the tent and lay down on the spruce.

Half an hour later when I turned in myself Joe was sound asleep.

I am glad he didn't know, as I know now, that on the night of the 22nd of August 1945 the nearest bad weather was over Indiana and was moving *away* from us and that the only storm on the North American continent was in Florida, 1,500 miles off as the loon flies.

Back at the railway depot by the hotel the visitors were looking at the weather forecast, fastened with Scotch tape on the window. It read "Fair to-day and to-morrow."

Next morning when I looked out of the tent there were unmistakable signs of a hot day ahead.

It was almost an exact replica of our first morning in Burnt Island Lake, the same low white mist over the water and the same signs that the sky was clear above. Patches of trees on the opposite shore were just visible, like islands in the mist, and the trees around the camp were covered in dewy tiaras, reflecting the filtered light from the sun above. At first it looked as if only one tree was thus decorated, but when you shifted your position you could see others, then more until every fir in sight stood revealed as a glistening, bejewelled Christmas tree. From the top downwards, every one was festooned with spiders' webs on which the night dew had settled to glisten in the morning light.

166

CHAPTER XIII

EVEN Joe had to admit it was "a peach of a morning." We were on the water at 10 o'clock, in weather so warm that we sat in our shirt-sleeves. The mash that had been so vibrant with life at night was a sweltering, tropical swamp. Crocodiles and hippos would have been more in keeping than beavers. There were plenty of birds, but for the animals it was the morning after the night before and they were sleeping the day away to freshen themselves for the coming dusk.

Joe said the place to look for a moose or deer was at the edges of the mash, where the bush came down to the water. If any were there, we didn't see them. All we came across were cranes, snipe and ducks. We also found in the shallow water two balls of jelly, each the size of a melon. "Frog's eggs," said Joe. I never heard of frogs that could lay eggs that size, so I fished one up with the paddle to examine it more closely. The outside was rough and lumpy and cutting it in half I found the inside was hollow and full of water. It wasn't one egg but thousands, joined together in a ball. Our English frogs are not so tidy when they spawn. They leave the stuff about in shapeless messes that small boys collect in jam jars. What a thrill my schoolfellows and I would have had if we'd discovered one of these monstrous jelly-balls in an English pond. We'd have driven everyone mad by trying to hatch it in the bath.

As we progressed through the mash I saw how right Joe was to turn back when he did the previous night, for even in daylight, with a map spread open on my knees, it was difficult not to get lost in this maze of waterways. After a couple of hours' hard work in the open swamp the hills closed in on each side and the stream became little more than a trickle of water, a few feet wide. Joe hadn't been this way for many years and the heat, plus the difficulty of paddling when the canoe was resting on the mud half the time, made him swear he would never come again. Half a mile before arriving at the established portaging-place I had to get out to lighten the canoe. Jack the Ranger, who came this way every Saturday on his way home, had cut a track through the brush for just such an emergency and I followed this on foot while Joe punted the canoe through the slime.

The first portage was a tough one, 848 yards according to the map, and most of it uphill. I badly miscalculated the half-way mark and dumped the first load after going only a third of the way. I paced out 515 steps and thought that must be a good half, but I either counted wrong or my steps were shorter than I imagined, for the second part was 738 paces. It was hotter than ever in the woods and we were hardly on speaking terms when we reloaded the canoe at the far end.

It was only 150 yards from the end of this portage to the start of the next. The stream between was spring-fed and crystal clear as it wound between the rocks, green and mossy at the bottom and crowded with small fish. It was like looking down from a skyscraper on a busy city street. Most of the fish were perch, striped yellow and black like water tigers, and the bigger ones swam in front of the canoe in little groups of half a dozen. I thought it all very lovely but

Joe was hot, and hungry. The stream contained many submerged rocks into which we bumped constantly and each time we did so Joe got more annoyed. He said it was my fault because, from the bows of the canoe, I could see the rocks ahead and he couldn't. He was quite right, of course, so for the rest of the way to the portage I had to look out for sunken rocks instead of gazing at the fish and the scenery.

There was one thing about Joe, even on the hottest day he had only to get some food inside him and he was chirpy and cheery again in a few minutes. We had lunch beside the stream before making the second and final portage of the day, and after the first few mouthfuls he was back in his old form.

He said that when we got to McIntosh Lake, where we intended to stay for the last two nights of the trip, we would have to catch a fish at all costs, for the next day was Friday. This statement was followed by a long story, with many purple patches, of a girl he met in the bush when he was young who was "so good you would walk on water to get her." Their acquaintance ripened and then cooled and at that stage she asked him to marry her. When refused she said that if she died first she was going to light a special fire for him in hell.

"Well, sir, darned if she didn't up and die of a stroke last year and I guess she's busy in hell stoking up that fire for me right now, so you see I can't take no risks, such as eating meat stew on a Friday. We just has to catch a fish or I don't eat."

The next portage was nearly as hard work as the last one had been, but as I stumbled the final yards, almost blinded by my own sweat, spruce trees parted and ahead lay the sparkling blue water of McIntosh

Lake, which I shall remember until I die as one of the most beautiful spots on earth.

I suppose there are ten thousand lakes in Canada just as beautiful but this place is where I really lost my heart to the northern woodlands. It was the last word in peace and restfulness. Whoever Mr. McIntosh was, he has a memorial as lovely as the Taj Mahal. A dozen wooded islets studded the blue of the water and, round the edges, rocky bays and crooked little arms of water stretched their way between the trees. By the shore, where we came out from the woods, a temple of nature-carved rocks lay half submerged, shining in the sun above the water and shimmering below. The resident loons greeted us with old-world courtesy and dragon-flies (which Joe called "darning needles") buzzed among the water-lily blossoms like animated costume jewellery. And it was all ours. For two days and nights we had it to ourselves.

The island we chose for our camp was the centre one of a string of three spreading across the mile and a half width of the lake. The ranger had told us a young couple were camping there, but they were gone when we arrived and I wish to thank them here and now for the welcome they left behind. There wasn't a thing out of place. The open ground had been swept with a broom of spruce boughs. Not a can was in sight, nor a scrap of paper. The fireplace was neat, with kindling wood stacked beside it, ready for the next arrivals. In a tidy little pile on the table, protected from possible rain by a cover of birch bark, were porridge oats, half a can of corn syrup, pancake flour, saccharin, and a cande.

I hope those two people were on their honeymoon, for I can imagine no better place to spend one. I hope their affairs prosper and they go back to the same place, year after year, for another honeymoon. I hope they are blessed with thousands of children, as many sons as they wish and the rest little girls with blue eyes and dimples. I will go farther and hope their landlord reduces their rent, a rich aunt leaves them a fortune and the tax collector loses their address.

Even Joe agreed it was a good camp to come upon, though he had to point out, professionally, that it was a bad place to choose for a site.

"Look at those big pines all round," he said. "If there was to be a thunderstorm you wouldn't think it so good."

The rocks in front could not have been better for bathing had they been designed for that purpose alone. You could dive from them or walk into the water slowly. Round the corner, where it caught the sun, was a tiny beach of sand and a paddling-pool. The woods and open ground were thick with blueberries. There were so many I even picked them inside the tent that night, by just stretching out my hand as I lay in the blankets.

The one disturbing thing about the place was a small pocket mirror nailed to the trunk of a pine. I had brought no mirror, nor had Joe, and neither of us had shaved for a week. I knew what Joe looked like but I had not thought of my own appearance. Now I saw a man with a white beard looking out of the glass at me. It made me feel like Rip Van Winkle. I had gone into the woods with Joe feeling like a young man, a boy. With the outside world forgotten, time had stood still. Now I'd come back—with a white beard. The mirror was not to be ignored. A dozen times I found myself stealing glances at it. Joe noticed and said I had a beard on me like "a deerskin in the fall after it's been 'sheeved' ready for tanning."

While Joe was unloading the canoe and making the camp I walked the few yards across the island and sat on a sunny rock, absorbing this paradise of woodland and glittering water. Over the lake a fishhawk poised stationary in the air for a moment, then plummeted into the water and flew up again with something gleaming in its talons. According to Joe, fishhawks "memorise the fish like a snake memorises a frog." A black and white nuthatch, seeking insects in a birch tree, crawled down the trunk head first to take a look at me and then went on with its bug hunt. A sudden whirr of tiny wings made me instinctively raise my arm to ward off what I thought was a bee till I found myself clutching at a humming bird. Just off the island a loon, having decided we were harmless, had brought its small brown son along for diving lessons among the minnows. It was so pleasant sitting there in the sun that when Joe called across that it was time to go fishing I wished that the morrow was any day but Friday.

At one time I had a nice trout on the line and brought it up to the side of the canoe but it escaped from the hook a second before Joe grabbed it. It was no more my fault than his, but Joe looked at me as if I was conspiring with the Devil and the lady in hell.

After another hour of it I would have been quite content to have given up fishing for the evening and tried again in the morning, but Joe kept suggesting new places and I felt for the sake of his immortal soul I had to go on. One stretch of deep water we tried was in front of the largest of the lake's islands. Joe said

there was a bear on it. He could hear him in the
bush. I asked how he got there. Did he swim?

"Of course he swimmed," said Joe. "You don't
think he flew, do you, like your foxes in Australia?
Every animal can swim. Even bats can swim. I've seen
'em. You're so smart, can you name any Jeezly animal
that can't?"

"How about the fisher?" I said. "You said he didn't
like the water."

"I never said it couldn't swim," he replied. "I said
it was like a cat and didn't like the water. A cat can
swim if it has to and so can an old fisher. All animals
can swim if they have to."

"Well, then," I said, "how about a pig?"

Nine people out of 10 will tell you that pigs can't
swim. Their front legs are so short and their hoofs
so sharp that they cut their own throats when they
try. I belong to the minority of one in 10 who know
that pigs *can* swim and I know because as a youth I
put the matter to the test. I had gone to Australia under an immigration scheme for boys and been sent to
a farm in Queensland, where several hundred pigs ran
half wild. Some of them sunbathed on the mud at
the edge of a large dam in which I and the other
hired hand sometimes bathed. We conceived the idea
of swimming up, very quietly, to the edge of the mud,
grabbing a couple of sleeping pigs by the hind legs
and dragging them back 10 or 20 yards into the
dam. We thought it good dirty fun in those days, but
it did teach us that pigs could swim. The old bachelor
who employed us had other practices with pigs to
which, I am pleased to say, neither of us young hands
subscribed. One took place at meal times, when the
bolder, half-grown pigs came right into our shanty

and looked up at us like dogs. If one came near enough to him the old man poured a cup of hot tea on its rump. Nothing whatever happened for two seconds and then, the heat having soaked through its thick hide, the pig jumped six inches in the air and dashed out of doors shrieking blue murder. In all humility I am bound to confess that it was very funny.

Joe happened to be another of the minority who know that pigs can swim. I had asked him only to hear what he would say, and what he said was this:

"Of course the old pig can swim. There's people in the bush who ought to know better, who says he cuts his throat if he tries it. Maybe it happened once and people got to talking about it and now you find everybody believing it's true. But I know it isn't. My old grandfather, the Indian, had two pigs on his farm that used to go for a swim round the lake every afternoon, and darn good swimmers they were."

The names of other unlikely swimmers occur. How about a kangaroo? Can you imagine it, with those enormous hind legs and tiny front paws? And a camel? I've heard the hump makes them top heavy and they overbalance. Cows, unlikely as it may seem, can swim. I have seen them do it in Norway, a whole herd of them, and a very pukka sahib I know says elephants are dashed good swimmers; but what about a bison? Or a giraffe?

I didn't think it worth mentioning these creatures to Joe. He would only have quoted flying foxes again.

One of the questions I sent to the Zoo was: "Are there any wild animals that cannot swim?" and the answer was "No." I asked Doktor Kuenen, who said, "The specific gravity of all animals is in the nature of

174

one, and it therefore requires little effort on their part to keep afloat. Some animals with an unusual centre of gravity, like the kangaroo you mention, may find it difficult but I do not imagine that any creature finds it impossible."

There you are. Joe and the scientists are in agreement but I think I would still want to see a kangaroo swim before being wholly convinced. I have read that a moor-hen, the common English moor-hen, can swim from the moment it comes out of the egg, but that, I know, is not true. Once, when I was punting on the Thames, I found a moor-hen's nest in which there was a chick half emerged from its egg. I completed the operation and put the chick in the water. Did it swim? It did not. It didn't sink, but it floated about so awkwardly that I am sure it would have drowned had I not lifted it out and returned it to the nest.

We were still fishing unsuccessfully when the sun went down. A quarter of a mile away was a long straight stretch of shore, with the spruce and hemlocks right down to the water and from it, without warning, came the howl of a wolf. I didn't need Joe to tell me what it was. That long-drawn, eerie sound, rising to a crescendo of misery and tapering off into something like a sob, could be nothing else. The wolf was answered by another and another until there were half a dozen of them at it, and the farthest not half a mile away. At the first sound Joe forgot all about the fish. The wolves were howling, winter was coming and he was elated.

We pulled in the line and returned to the island. Another pack on the other side of the lake had started howling, too, and I felt devoutly thankful we had chosen to camp on an island.

Joe said wolves never attack anybody, but I come from Europe where a wolf ate Red Riding Hood's grandmother—and you never know.

"The Government once offered 1,000 bucks to anyone who could prove he'd been attacked by a wolf in Canada," Joe said. "There was many slick fellows from the city tried to get the money, but none of them succeeded. They had to tell their story to a board, and there was an old bushman sitting there who caught them all out. They thought they would just have to come along with a witness who'd say he saw them attacked and they'd get the money. By the time that old man had finished questioning them they wished they'd never come.

"Mind you, *I* could have proved I was attacked by a wolf, but I wouldn't have got the money because the wolf was my own. I dug it out of a hole as a pup and reared it. My grandfather was in hospital and when he came out grandmother said to him, 'I don't like Joe's wolf. It always follows him and won't go ahead. The granddad says, "That's bad, Joe. Youse ought to get rid of him. One day you'll trip and fall and he'll jump on you.' Well, sir, I thought I'd see, and so I took a walk in the woods with the wolf and when he was about 10 yards behind I threw my hat and coat on the ground and hopped behind a hemlock. That wolf was so quick I hardly see'd him move. He just gave one leap and he was on the coat. Then he looked up at me, standing there behind the hemlock with my gun ready. The look in his eyes, sir, wasn't like the pup I reared. It was the look of a wild animal."

Joe shot it, right between the eyes, with their foiled traitorous look.

Three times in his life, Joe said, wolves had attacked

his dog team, but they never harmed him. Once he was sledging across a lake with stores for a mining camp. As he passed near a headland a gang of wolves came out and tore the dog team to bits before Joe could get them loose. It took him all night to walk back. After that the mining company he was working for gave him a rifle and next time he passed the same spot he gave it a slightly wider berth so as to have more time to shoot as the wolves came out.

"I picked them off, one by one, as they came from the trees. Not one of them ever got out to me," said Joe.

They may not be very hair-raising stories, these, but real live wolves were howling half a mile away as Joe told them and I felt thoroughly creepy.

This was the night of the August full moon—the "Jobber's sun" Joe called it as it rose, yellow and huge, between two black pines standing out above the others on the shore. Round the island the minnows were jumping, plunk, plunk, every few seconds and all the time the wolves went on howling. One of them had what Joe called a "voice on him like a train whistle." I tried to time him. His howl lasted two to four seconds and then echoed round the woods for several seconds more. From time to time the loons joined in and then the row was really frightful.

That night, too, saw the northern lights again, so what with that and the wolves Joe was in very high spirits.

It was a beautifully warm and balmy evening but the spell was on Joe again and he piled the fire high with logs. This drove the wolves farther away, but they continued to howl in the middle distance all night.

They form up ino gangs of 40 or 50 when winter approaches, said Joe, and they will come right up to the houses and howl, making pans rattle on their hooks. Joe had a great respect for wolves. As a bush dweller himself he admired their cunning and woodcraft; amongst other thingss, he said, a wolf has the best eyesight of any animal in the bush.

"Not a lynx?" I queried.

"A lynx?" he said in surprise. "No, sir, I never heard that a lynx could see far."

From wolves I got Joe talking about dogs. He had the best dog team in the district, he said. The leader was a collie, yes a collie, with the name of "Driver." He would have liked a whole team of collies. They had the best brains of any dog he knew, but were a lot of trouble as they had to wear moccasins in winter. The hair between their toes freezes, and in trying to bite the ice out they tear their feet till they bleed.

After the collie leader, he had six Newfoundland dogs. They cost him 45 dollars a piece as pups. They were named Jack, Nigger, Fido, Schneider (" so called because he's such a son of a gun"), Queenie, and Snowball (curious name for a black dog). He didn't like huskies. He thought them treacherous and had had to shoot a couple in his time. A sledge dog is good for three seasons, then it begins to stiffen up.

The lake and the wooded islands were so lovely in the moonlight that I sat on a rock gazing at them for an hour after the fire had died out and Joe gone to bed. A hundred yards away another little island caught the full light of the moon and away in the south the piled masses of a thunder-cloud were lit up, almost as if by the sun. The wolves were still howling at intervals in the distance and the echoing loons were answering when I pulled off my shirt and trousers and slid into the lake. There was no current and no wind and after the first sting the water was warm and soft. I swam to the island opposite and sat naked and wet on a long-dead log. Some animal scurried along the stones behind as I dangled my feet in the water. Across the little strait I could see the outline of our canoe, drawn up on the rocks, and the white of our tent, half hidden by the pines. I could even make out my clothes, last contact with civilised man and his ways, piled on the rock where they had been dropped. It was like escaping into space and looking back with detachment at the earth to which all your life you have been bound; or a soul surveying the body from which it had departed. The wolves went on howling and the moon, casting its pale light on the water and rocks, made them look part of a world to which I did not belong.

Have you ever felt like a ghost, suspended between two existences and owned by neither?

I was not in Valhalla with so many of my friends and I wasn't on earth. My clothes and the camp over there seemed symbolic of something to which I had to get back, or I was lost. In the panic to return I flayed the water with my arms and legs and found comfort in the sound I was making. All the loons on the lake woke up and began to wail and Joe came from the tent to see what the row was about. I built a huge fire and asked Joe to stay, for I had to talk and be talked to. There are people I have known all my life who would have scoffed at these fancies but Joe, the Indian I'd known but a week, understood without explanation.

We sat round the fire for another hour while he told

me that it was not only people that became ghosts, but the animals and the trees as well.

"There's many don't know this," he said, "but the winds and the rain and the lightning is all ghosts too. I know because I've heard them talking when I was alone in the bush. I'm not afraid of being a ghost, because it's natural. A ghost's only a spirit which hasn't no body any more and all things has spirits. The bad thing would be if they hadn't. You wait and see; if I die first I'll come and haunt you and you won't find it anything to be scared at."

"I'd never be frightened of your ghost, Joe," I said.

We both laughed and went to bed.

The loons settled down but the wolves in the distance howled till dawn.

CHAPTER XIV

MEATLESS Friday dawned fair, with a moderate south-west wind, and immediately after breakfast we set off fishing. We trolled for an hour without any luck and then the wind turned westerly and became too strong for us to stay with safety on the main part of the lake. After trying one or two sheltered spots we gave up because the troll kept hooking itself on the bottom. It began to look as if Joe would have to eat beans for lunch.

I went off on my own to catch some minnows for bait while Joe sat around the camp looking miserable. There was a sheltered corner among the rocks on the sunny side of the island and the bread paste was deadly. In a few minutes I had a pailful of minnows which I took to Joe and suggested he should cook them like sprats. He did not fancy the idea, so I went back to the rocks and went on fishing for the fun of it, putting the minnows back as I caught them. There was a shoal of small fry near the surface and below them a dozen big fellows several inches long. The moment I dropped in the bait one of the big ones shot up, scattering the fry as he came, and grabbed the paste. The small fellows were not considered at all, but the others seemed to have a co-lateral agreement among themselves, for two of them never went for the bait at the same time. There was one regular Hitler of a minnow who seemed to have special privileges. I caught him again and again, proving that it was the same one by trying cotton round the base of his tail before throwing him back. For a minute or two he sulked among the rocks but he soon found his confidence again and came back. As Joe would have said, nature is natural. It is only among people that such behaviour is called "aggression," "greed" or "free enterprise."

The wind stayed strong, but I discovered, by casting with a weight from the island, that there was deep water a few yards out. We were able to troll backwards and forwards there, in the shelter of the land, without going near the main lake. In half an hour we landed two trout and lost four, fishing 20 feet down with a dead minnow. The fish behaved in a peculiar way. Instead of taking the bait with a rush, as a good trout should do, they nibbled at it. I would feel a strike, think I'd lost the fish, feel it again, start to wind in, be quite certain it was gone, continue to wind in to renew the bait and then find the fish had followed all the way up to the surface. Joe swore he saw one of these trout let go the bait and attack the copper line in front.

The two fish we did catch were a remarkable contrast. They were both about 18 inches long yet one was nearly twice as heavy as the other. Joe called the thin one a "starveling" and said it hadn't eaten for weeks. There was a wound in its head where it might have carried a hook.

"He's been working hard to get rid of that hook, that's what it is," Joe said. "It takes a fish four days to lose a hook. Never less, never more. The flesh and the bone rots where the point goes in and he works the end about on the bottom till it comes out. It's mighty hard work and he don't feel too good at the end of it."

Joe wouldn't eat the starveling. I thought that as we had killed it we ought at least to make a gesture and I cooked it myself. It was edible, but that was about all.

It was as well we caught our fish when we did, because in the afternoon the wind grew so strong that we began to wonder again if we were to be marooned on an island. This time it would be more serious because my leave ended at midnight on Sunday and somehow or other I must get back to Washington by then, if I had to swim the lake and walk through the woods to the railway.

All afternoon the great cumulus cloud lavers piled up, with misty stratus scudding below. Through occasional gaps we could see a mackerel sky above. The pine trees round the camp creaked in the wind and an undertone of rustling came from the drying leaves of the brush. Joe moved into the tent and wrapping himself in a blanket went to sleep. I tried to pass the time catching more minnows. There was no sheltered corner to sit this time, the sun had gone and so had the minnows.

The island was no more than 50 yards across and in half an hour I had explored it thoroughly. The only find of interest was a pile of empty clam shells in the shallows. There are many of these piles in the lakes. Joe said they were made by muskrats who opened the clams with their teeth.

When it grew too cold to sit around any longer I, too, rolled up in my blanket and went to sleep.

We ate our supper huddled round the fire and Joe chose this time to tell me how to store ice for the summer. You cut the blocks from the lake in March and chip them till they are about a foot square and all blue ice. They should be piled in the ice house with eight inches of sawdust at the sides and a foot on top. More sawdust than this generates heat and melts the ice. Some people put sawdust between the layers of ice, but that was a refinement Joe considered unnecessary.

In the winter when he went trapping he made hollows in the ice of the lake and froze his potatoes, turnips and carrots. Bread can also be kept fresh if it is frozen. I always thought potatoes were ruined if the frost got at them, but Joe said they are all right if you let them stay frozen till you need them. Then you put them into cold water and cook slowly. If put straight in hot water they turn black and if allowed to thaw before use they go bad.

The wind calmed down about 10 that evening and

I suggested that we pack up and paddle to the mainland while we could. Then, if the weather got worse, we wouldn't be marooned in the morning. Joe agreed it would be a good plan, but he was suffering from his "innergestion" and did not feel up to the work involved. I thought at the time this was just an excuse for staying comfortably in camp where we were instead of paddling across the lake and setting up again in the dark. As I felt rather lazy myself I didn't press the matter.

No rain fell during the night, and in the morning the lake was misty and calm. By seven a south-west wind had shifted the mist from the water, blowing it into the surrounding hill valleys where it hung like smoke. The eggs and the bacon had gone and Joe made pancakes with the mixture we inherited from the previous campers. We ate them with syrup, and before we'd had time to clear up the table and wash the dishes it began to rain.

Our train was due at Brulé Lake somewhere around six in the evening. To get there we had two portages of about half a mile each, a shorter one, and four lakes to cross. Joe reckoned it would take us three to four hours. Around half-past ten we saw Jack the Ranger and his wife crossing the lake in the rain, on their way to Brulé for the week-end.

"Hell!" said Joe "if a woman can take it, we can. We'll show them we're not made of sugar."

When we came to fold the sodden tent it was just as Joe had said before we started. It weighed nearly as much as all the rest of our kit together. On previous portages I had carried it on top of one of the packs. Now, alone, the tent was as heavy as two packs.

In our haste to show "we were not made of sugar"

we did not leave the camp quite as tidy as we found it, I'm afraid, but at least there were no tins, rags or paper lying about. All the food we didn't want we put under the table, covered with bark strips, for Jack the Ranger to pick up next time he came through. We packed up the camp in about 20 minutes and got very wet doing it. Then it stopped raining. If we had smoked another cigarette before taking down the tent we'd have stayed dry.

After the first portage came Straight Shore Lake, narrow and about a mile long. Half-way down was a clearing in the bush and there we saw a doe and her speckled fawn, up to their knees in the water. The doe left the water when she saw us, and stood behind some bushes where we could see her head peeping anxiously round, but the fawn, like a naughty child that won't come out of the rain when he's called, went on nibbling at the beaver bush on the bank. In her anxiety the mother couldn't keep still. She trotted half-way into the clearing, looking round all the time to see if the errant offspring was following. The fawn took not the slighest notice of either her or us, as we paddled silently by. He might have been saying, "This stupid mother of mine, making all this fuss when there is good beaver bush to be had for the nibbling! Why do women always want you to do something else, just when you are enjoying yourself?"

Unable to stand the agony of suspense any longer the mother returned to the water and almost pushed the little fellow to the bank. There he turned round and looked at us and then, slowly, like a child who knows it has to obey but by obeying hopes to expose the foolishness of the order, he stalked, with head high, into the bush to join his mother.

Our last lake before Brulé was called Rosswood. It was a perfect little picture-book lake, a mile long and a few hundred yards wide, and at the far end lay a lily pool as serene and beautiful as any we had seen, with a stream trickling out through a beaver dam into the woods. I kept looking back at it as we dragged the canoe on to a landing-stage of rotting wood for the last portage. And I was glad of the second load so that I could return to it alone for a last look. Brulé Lake has a railway running along one side, it has a sawmill, and houses are scattered round the shore. Comparatively speaking, it is civilisation. Rosswood was the last bit of the wilds I would see and I approached it for the second time silently picking my steps so that I would not surprise it in its beauty.

I could hear a bullfrog croaking among the lily pads before I could see the water itself. Bees were searching for late summer honey in a tall patch of purple flowers that looked like Michaelmas daisies. To the left was the lake; to the right, the beaver dam and the stream; and ahead, the lily pool with the forest behind. There among the blossoms and the floating leaves would have been the perfect place to see a moose, and this the perfect moment. He would be standing sideways on to me and look as big as a house. I could see the exact spot among the lilies where he ought to be. The water would be above his hoofs and the velvet on his growing antlers would have begun to peel so that it hung down in strips. Drooping from the corner of his mouth there might be a half-chewed lily root, plucked from the bottom and still dripping water. At sight of me he would stop chewing and stare back, flicking his ears and extending his nostrils inquiringly. What would happen then? Would he turn with dignity and stalk off into the woods? Or crash away in a panic, regardless of the noise he was making? Some day I must return and find out.

With the remaining packs loaded on my back I resolutely turned away from Rosswood Lake and what the practical Commissioner of the Mounted Police would call "the figment of my imagination."

Throughout the trip I had been so confident we would meet a moose that instead of asking Joe more about them I intended leaving my questions until after we had seen one. We lunched at the edge of Brulé Lake, and I tried to make up for lost time by asking Joe to talk about moose.

In Ontario, he said, they were protected all the year round, but across the border in Quebec there was still a short open season. A dressed moose about five years old provides 15 to 16 cwts. of good red meat, enough to last a family all the winter, so the temptation to disregard the law is strong.

Once Joe came across a place in the bush where two bull moose had been fighting. An acre of ground had been trampled down in the battle and there was moose hair in all the trees. In the centre of the arena was one of the bulls, resting after the fight, and, as Joe approached, it got to its feet with the hair on its neck rising in anger. A bull moose in the breeding-season is a dangerous animal and Joe said he was taking no chances. He fired as it rose and the bullet grazed the spine without cutting the skin. It was sufficient to knock the moose unconscious and Joe dispatched it with a hunting-knife. He thus found himself with an entire winter's supply of meat, and a moose hide without so much as a bullet hole in it. He cached the meat on an island in the river near his home and hid the skin in a shed. The head he left in the bush.

"But," said Joe, "there's what they call a stool pigeon in every Jeezer town, and before long the rangers came round to the house. I said, 'Yes, I have a hide and a supply of meat but I haven't killed a moose. I came on two moose in the bush,' I said, 'and their horns was locked together, as sometimes happens. One of them was dead and the other would have died too if I hadn't released it. So, you see,' I said to the rangers, 'I didn't kill a moose to get this meat, I saved the life of one.' "

He brought the skin for inspection and there was no mark on it, except a few hairs missing on the back, and that might have been done in the fight. He offered to take the rangers to the scene of the battle and show them the head, for he knew they would find no bullet marks in that either. " 'How far is it?' they asked. 'About two days' journey,' I said. They didn't fancy making a trip like that and left me with my hide and meat for the winter." The moral of the story? There isn't one, but it helps to explain why I, and thousands like me, have never seen a wild moose. If a deer provided 15 cwts. of meat instead of 150 pounds, I might not have seen a wild deer either.

We paddled the last mile across Brulé Lake escorted by Jack's schooboy son who had come out to meet us in a 14-foot canoe. Joe and he kept up a running conversation about the trip. Where had we been? What had we seen? How many fish did we catch? What was the biggest? Joe had answers for everything, not always strictly according to the facts but suitable for a boy spending his school holidays in the woods.

"Well, sir," Joe said to the schoolboy, "I have a fishing lure in my pack that is made from a cigarette case I took off a dead German. Clever people, Germans, clever, but ugly. I have a thing I took off another dead German. . . ."

There were a hundred questions I should have asked Joe, to fill in the gaps in our experience, but for him it was clearly over. He was starting his repertoire again at the beginning.

Jack, sitting on the veranda with his family, dried and bathed and changed, waved to us as we pulled our canoe from the water by the old sawmill. He shouted some crack, which I didn't catch, and Joe called back. Then we were humping out kit to the station on the other side of the mill. We arrived with the last load at 3.25 p.m. by my watch. What I thought was a tiny red squirrel ran across the track.

"Chipmunk," said Joe.

I'd known about chipmunks from the cradle but, like so many things on the trip, this was the first I'd ever seen.

"It's very small," I said.

"Not when he's safe in a clump of hazel bush, he isn't," said Joe. "He talks then as if he was the biggest fellow in the bush."

That was the last wild creature we saw and the last of Joe's observations on natural history. At 3.30 the rain came down, sheets of it, the rain that Joe had been predicting ever since we started, the sort that young reporters describe as "a tropical downpour."

Joe was pleased. He would have been more pleased if he had known that this time he was right and the experts wrong. For the official forecast for the locality was "scattered showers, clearing in the afternoon."

Two railwaymen came tearing down the track on a "pumper," whipped it off the lines and joined us in the shelter of the bare wooden waiting-room, stamping the water from their boots. Joe, with a new audience, took out the fishing lure made from the German cigarette case.

"Curse the bush," said one of the railwaymen. "I hate every minute of it. I won't be happy till the company send me back to a section in the city. Any city, so long as there are houses and not trees."

Joe persisted with his story of the fishing lure and by sheer force of character got the railwaymen interested. Quite suddenly I felt very tired and if wishes could have transported me back to the bar in New York where it all began, I would have been there instead of sitting on the floor with my coat collar turned up to keep the draught from my neck. It was all right for Joe, he belonged to the woods so securely that civilisation could not shake his spirit. The first war caught him up as an illiterate Indian and he emerged with a medal; the "great compression" ruined lesser men but left Joe with his values unchanged, the end of the second war saw him return to the woods unscathed after helping to build an atomic bomb factory.

But I sat there with a stiff neck and soaked to the skin; the rain splashed through a hole in the roof and fell in cold drops on my face. I had an eight-day beard and hadn't had a hot bath or a drink for a week. It went on raining all evening and the train was three hours late.

Next morning we went our destined ways; I bound for England, civvy street and a city desk; Joe to the woods again to catch up a party that had started without him. Throughout the following winter I often thought of him up there in the snow, setting his beaver traps and listening to the wolves. At times the picture was so clear that he seemed to materialise in the office beside me and say, "What a Jeezly place to find you." I sometimes wondered if these visitations were more than fancy, and then in the spring I learned that Joe had died a few weeks after our trails had crossed.

THE END